FEW AND CHOSEN

Defining Cardinal Greatness Across the Eras

Tim McCarver

with Phil Pepe

TRIUMPH
BOOKS
CHICAGO

Library of Congress Cataloging-in-Publication Data

McCarver, Tim.
    Few and chosen : defining Cardinal greatness across the eras / Tim McCarver and Phil Pepe.
      p. cm.
    Includes index.
    ISBN 1-57243-483-X (hc)
    1. St. Louis Cardinals (Baseball team)—History 2. Baseball players—Rating of—United States. I. Pepe, Phil. II. Title.

GV875.S3 M39 2003
796.357'64'0977866—dc21

2002514115

This book is available in quantity at special discounts for your group or organization. For further information, contact:

Triumph Books
601 South LaSalle Street
Suite 500
Chicago, Illinois 60605
(312) 939-3330
Fax (312) 663-3557

Printed in the United States of America
ISBN 1-57243-483-X
Interior design by Nick Panos

This book is dedicated to the more than 1,800 players, coaches, and managers who have worn the Cardinals uniform from 1892 to the present, and to the many voices who broadcast Cardinals games throughout the years, especially the late, great Hall of Famer, Jack Buck.

Contents

Foreword

I KNOW THAT IF I WAS strolling through my local bookstore and ran across a book of the best of the best Cardinals to ever play, I would put it down immediately and walk directly to the magazine rack. If I was in the right mood, however, and I did pick it up and realized that these choices were made by this guy McCarver, who has seen every Cardinal play all the way back to Jake Beckley and was a teammate of most of them, I might let my fingers do the walking.

My nature is to think of my favorite players and then see where they rank in the history of the organization. If you are like me, then let's be honest; it doesn't matter how many players are covered in this book. If you are just looking for your favorites, there is a chance that you will finish it unsatisfied and maybe a little angry.

How can I say this about a book written by a baseball historian like Tim? I say it because my list of favorite Cardinals is not at all like yours, or hers, or his. I bet without reading an advance copy of this piece of work that Dave LaPoint is not mentioned. I would also assume that Doug Rader did not make the index either. If I made a list of *my* all-time top ten "birds on bat" wearers, those names, as well as the names of such immortals as Tony Scott and Roger Freed, would be there.

Want to know something else? Tim McCarver's name wouldn't make the cut. It couldn't. He doesn't qualify. Stan Musial? Dizzy Dean? Rogers Hornsby? No chance. This doesn't mean that I don't respect their accomplishments. God knows I have to hear from Tim over and over every

Saturday during the summer about how underrated he was, or how Bob Gibson was nothing without him. That's just a joke. Tim would never say that about Gibson. Steve Carlton, maybe, but not Gibson.

The point is, I cannot consider anyone who played before I was born a favorite Cardinal of mine.

My list starts around 1974 (I was five years old then) and, in a way, ends in the late eighties. How can it end? How come Tino Martinez will never be on my list even though he is a terrific player and person? Well, to me, the players I idolized as a kid will always hold a special place in my heart.

No matter how much I think I know about the game these days, those days hanging around the park were different. My guys, no matter how irrelevant they are in the overall history of the game, were front and center in my world as a kid. They became like extended members of my family. Even though I had a privileged youth because of the position my father, Jack, had with the club, I would imagine this holds true for most fans.

I grew up hearing about the Gashouse Gang, Terry Moore, Stan the Man, and so on. Although I am proud that these players were Cardinals and are considered among the best in the game's rich history, I really can't rank their abilities compared to others during their time; or other generations, for that matter. I am jealous of those who grew up in the fifties and sixties. They got to call Stan and Red and Gibby boyhood idols. That was an era of baseball I wish I could have witnessed. Instead, I got the seventies. What do they say about timing? We got Ted Simmons and not much else. Then came the eighties, with Keith, Willie, and Ozzie.

The latest generation enjoyed Big Mac and the home run chase of 1998. A lot of people will claim those memories as life changing and unforgettable, but again, to me it's the kids who lived through that season and through all that McGwire did in a Cardinals uniform who really got the most from those summer nights.

Maybe I'm wrong, but when you are a kid, the game just seems pure. I never heard of one kid bothering to figure out how much McGwire made per home run. They didn't care how the cash-strapped Oakland Athletics had to trade him to the Cardinals in 1997 because the A's couldn't afford to compete with the multimillion-dollar offers he was sure to get in the open market. They just knew he was a larger-than-life figure who represented their favorite team by belting gargantuan home runs with a wink to his own son and an eye on history.

Those of us in St. Louis consider ourselves the best baseball fans in the country. I don't know if we are. I do know that, as a whole, Cardinals fans seem to appreciate baseball played the right way more than most. Cardinals fans can be found all across the map. Geography and baseball's slow expansion to the west have a lot to do with that, as does the strength of the Cardinals radio network.

I have seen the power of Cardinals baseball my whole life, trailing around after my dad. He was at least one of the Cardinals voices from 1954 to 2001. The power of Cardinals baseball to affect lives throughout the Midwest and beyond is truly awesome. From one spring to the next, from one generation to the other, the Cardinals link what was to what is. Through the years, the names and personalities change, but the people that line up on that first-base line in early April star in one long show that runs from spring through the end of summer.

So, what is the best baseball franchise in history? Well, I do believe that there is as much pride for Cardinals history among their faithful as there is for the vaunted Yankees by their followers. There is no debating that the New York franchise is the most successful in professional sports history. But that's New York, the biggest city in the world, the city that never sleeps. In the Midwest, we sleep. We go to work, we come home, and we go to bed. When baseball season is in full swing, however, that changes. The Cardinal Nation is alive and the city hops when the ball is flying around Busch. No, the Cardinals don't have as many world championships as the Yankees, but so what? I have always contended that the Cardinals are like the NFL's Green Bay Packers a small-market team with wide national appeal built on success and the classy way the organization has been run.

It's fun for all of us Cardinals fans to argue who is the best at each position. But, if you are not a Cardinals fan, know this: if you start yappin' about how Williams, Mays, or A-Rod is the best ever and you ignore the Cardinals greats, beware! You're messin' with family.

I hope you enjoy the book! About that first line, I was just kidding. I always like to get a rise out of Tim. I was honored when I was asked to write this Foreword. It is the first time I have done something like this. By finishing my part, I now have written more Forewords than I have read.

—JOE BUCK
St. Louis, Missouri

Preface

In the colorful jargon of baseball, a catcher's equipment—mask, mitt, chest protector, and shin guards—is known as "the tools of ignorance," a tongue-in-cheek term that is, in reality, a misnomer.

Considering that, of the 30 men managing major league teams at the start of the 2002 season, 8 (27 percent) plied their trade as catchers (Bruce Bochy in San Diego, Mike Scoscia in Anaheim, Buck Martinez in Toronto, Bob Boone in Cincinnati, Jeff Torborg in Florida, Jerry Narron in Texas, and the two 2001 World Series managers, Joe Torre of the Yankees and Bob Brenly of the Diamondbacks), I submit that the catching gear is anything but "the tools of ignorance."

Except for the pitcher (who works once every four or five days if he's a starter, a few innings a week if he's a reliever) the catcher is the only player on the field who is active on every pitch on defense. He also is involved as part of the offense, in some cases (Yogi Berra, Johnny Bench, Mickey Cochrane, Bill Dickey, Gabby Hartnett, Mike Piazza) a very important part.

Throughout the history of baseball, catchers have distinguished themselves as among the more cerebral participants in the game, as managers and executives.

Branch Rickey, considered by many the most astute of all baseball thinkers, the father of the farm system, played four major league seasons as a catcher prior to becoming a manager, general manager, and all-around baseball guru.

The legendary Connie Mack spent 11 years as a catcher before becoming the granddaddy of all managers. He managed more games (7,878), won more games (3,776), and lost more games (4,025) than any other manager in baseball history. He also was on the job as a manager for an incredible 53 years, 50 of them with one team, the Philadelphia Athletics. Of course, he owned the team, proving his intelligence.

Some of the greatest managers in baseball history were catchers. Yogi Berra, Bill Carrigan, Mickey Cochrane, Gil Hodges, Ralph Houk, Darrell Johnson, Al Lopez, Steve O'Neill, Wilbert Robinson, Buck Rodgers, Luke Sewell, and Gabby Street, all catchers, were pennant-winning managers. Although they never won a pennant, former catchers Bobby Bragan, Roger Bresnahan, Del Crandall, Herman Franks, Paul Richards, Bob Scheffing, and Birdie Tebbetts were regarded as excellent managers.

Catchers have been in demand as baseball radio and television analysts as well. Joe Garagiola, a catcher for the St. Louis Cardinals, Pittsburgh Pirates, Chicago Cubs, and New York Giants in the forties and fifties, was a pioneer in going from the playing field to the broadcast booth, paving the way for a stream of catchers-turned-broadcasters that today includes Bob Uecker, Kevin Kennedy, Bob Montgomery, Jim Price, Ray Fosse, Alex Trevino, and Alan Ashby.

The premier catcher-turned-broadcaster is Tim McCarver, who played 21 seasons in the major leagues and has spent another two decades as a baseball broadcaster/analyst. In his 10 seasons with the Cardinals, McCarver played on three pennant winners and two World Series champions. His insight and perception of the game acquired in 21 years as a catcher would have made him a natural to manage a major league team. No doubt there were opportunities, but McCarver wisely resisted them all to remain in the broadcast booth for more than two decades.

St. Louis was a charter member of the National League in 1876, withdrew after the 1877 season, and reentered in 1892 as the Browns, later changing its name to the Perfectos. In 1899, they became the St. Louis Cardinals and they have been Cardinals ever since.

Some of the greatest and most colorful players in baseball history have worn the uniform of the Cardinals, from Stan the "Man" Musial to Dizzy Dean to Rogers Hornsby to the "Fordham Flash" Frank Frisch; from the Gashouse Gang of Pepper Martin to Enos "Country" Slaughter to Bob Gibson to Lou Brock and home run king Mark McGwire.

In 2002, Ozzie Smith, the Wizard of Shortstop, became the 37th player or manager who wore the Cardinals uniform to be inducted into the Baseball Hall of Fame at Cooperstown, New York.

The New York Yankees have won more pennants (38) and more World Series (26) than any other team in baseball. The St. Louis Cardinals are the best in the National League with 15 pennants (the Dodgers won 18, but nine were in Brooklyn, nine in Los Angeles, and the Giants won 16 pennants, 13 in New York and 3 in San Francisco) and nine World Series titles. In head-to-head World Series competition with the Yankees, the Cardinals hold a 3–2 edge.

With more than 40 years of experience as catcher and broadcaster, an appreciation and knowledge of the history and tradition of baseball, and a keen insight into the game, Tim McCarver is uniquely qualified to attempt the daunting task of selecting an all-time Cardinals team, five players at each position chosen in order of preference.

—PHIL PEPE
Englewood, New Jersey

Acknowledgments

T HE AUTHORS WISH TO acknowledge the many people who helped in the preparation of this book, especially Steve Carlton, Bob Gibson, Ralph Kiner, Marty Marion, Clete Boyer, Bill White, Stan Musial, and the late Enos Slaughter, who gave so generously of their time.

Our thanks, also, to Mark Momjian, Jennifer Unter, Ruth Garibaldi, and Mitch Rogatz, Tom Bast, Blythe Hurley, and all the good people at Triumph Books.

Introduction

M Y EARLIEST BASEBALL RECOLLECTION is the sound of Harry Caray's voice, broadcasting St. Louis Cardinals games in the forties and fifties. I was a kid in Memphis, Tennessee, a hotbed of Cardinals baseball, Memphis sitting 290 miles south of St. Louis along the Mississippi River.

Football was my favorite sport when I was a kid, but I was a big baseball fan, too. I wasn't a Cardinals fan, just a baseball fan, but because of Harry Caray, you couldn't help but follow the Cardinals.

When I was little, we played our own version of stickball. We would take a thermos cork and weight it down with pennies and nails. Then we'd hit that cork with an old broomstick, and I'd try to sound like Harry Caray broadcasting our games the way Harry broadcast Cardinals games.

You can't imagine the range in those days of radio station KMOX in St. Louis, which carried the Cardinals games. It drifted down from St. Louis through Arkansas, Oklahoma, and Texas, all the way south to the Mexican border. It ranged as far west as Denver and Arizona and into the south, through the Carolinas, Georgia, Alabama, and Florida. This was before there was major league baseball in Atlanta, Houston, and Florida, and Cardinals games on KMOX was all the major league baseball you could get. The entire South, Southwest, and much of the West were saturated with Cardinals baseball. As a result, next to the Yankees, the Cardinals were arguably the most popular team in the country. Not as rabid as the Dodgers following, but popular.

Until I was seven, I had a speech impediment, a lisp, and I had trouble pronouncing some words, but the repetitious sounds of consonants were easier for me to say. Stan Musial was a major impact player at the time and I was aware of him, but I didn't know much about him. Because of my speech problem, two Cardinals, Rip Repulski and Jabbo Jablonski, were my favorite players.

As far back as I can remember I was involved in sports. I was the next to youngest of five children, four boys and a girl. My sister, the second oldest, was a major influence on me. It was my sister, Marilyn, as in Monroe, who made me a left-handed hitter. I do everything right-handed except hit a baseball and that was Marilyn's idea.

"Everybody hits right-handed," she said. "Why don't you hit from the other side?"

When I was about three or four, Marilyn would get on her hands and knees and roll balls to me and have me hit them left-handed.

My father was a policeman, and he was active in sports. He umpired in the Rotary League and did a little coaching. He was a big influence in getting me to play ball. I used to go with my father when he umpired games in which my brothers played. My brothers played for a team called "Bemis Bags," but there was a team in the league, called "Oliver Finney," whose players were called the Candy Kids and one day only eight of their players showed up.

"You can use my youngest son, Tim," my father told the coach, Mr. Caldwell.

I was only eight at the time, but they would have forfeited the game if I didn't play, so they put me in right field. I was the only player without a uniform, but after the game I was given one. I was so proud of that uniform, sweat or not, and, yep, I slept in it. You couldn't get me out of it. From that day on, I was on the team. It was a 10- to 12-year-old league, and I was only 8. I played in that league for two years before I was eligible.

I saw my first Cardinals game, and my first major league game, when I was 10. Our team won our league championship and our reward was a trip to St. Louis to see the Cardinals play. I don't remember anything about the game. The only thing I remember is that we stayed in the Monteleone Hotel, across from St. Louis University. Water balloons dropped from the 10th floor were just too tempting and the peer pressure was too great.

The other thing I remember is having a team picture taken with Eddie Stanky. I still have the picture. I'm standing next to Stanky and I have a duck whistle in my mouth (duck whistles were very big with kids in Memphis at the time).

Memphis was a hotbed for baseball when I was young. We had a professional team in the Southern Association, the Memphis Chicks, named for the Chickasaw Indian tribe. They played their home games at Russwood Park, and when I was young I sold popcorn there, so I was able to see a lot of future major leaguers. Luis Aparicio, for example. I remember him because in 1954 he was the player with the darkest complexion in the Southern Association. I also got to see some major league teams who, in those days, would stop in Memphis, barnstorming north on their way home from spring training.

Years later, when I signed with the Cardinals, I was sent to Keokuk, Iowa, in my first year as a professional. The next year, when I was only 18, I played for Memphis, and was I ever excited with the prospect of playing baseball as a professional in the same ballpark in which I had earned a half cent a bag selling peanuts and popcorn. However, the ballpark burned down before the first game of the 1960 season.

As I said, when I was young, football was my favorite sport. I was an end on an outstanding football team at Christian Brothers High School and in my senior year, there was a lot of speculation in the local newspapers about whether I would go to college to play football or sign a baseball contract.

General Bob Neyland, the legendary coach at the University of Tennessee, wanted me, and he sent Johnny Majors, the great Tennessee running back, to recruit me. Moose Krause, athletic director at Notre Dame, invited a teammate, Buddy Soefker, and me to Notre Dame for their game against Purdue. It was October 24, 1958. I still have the ticket stubs.

After the game, Moose gave Buddy and me $10 each to go to a movie, probably a violation of NCAA rules.

There was some pressure on me to go to the University of Tennessee, and since I went to a Catholic high school, some pressure from the Christian Brothers for me to go to Notre Dame. But I never seriously considered going to Notre Dame because they told me, "If you come here, you must play football and baseball."

That kind of turned me off. They never actually offered me a scholarship, and besides, I had pretty much made up my mind that I was going to sign a baseball contract because of the money. The Cardinals offered me a $75,000 bonus, which was all the money in the world to me at the time. It was more money than my dad had made in his lifetime.

The Yankees and the Giants also were interested. Bill Dickey, the great Hall of Fame catcher, was the Yankees scout in our area. He lived in Little Rock, Arkansas, about 120 miles from Memphis, and he spent a lot of time trying to sign me. Bill was a great fisherman. In those days, Catholics could not eat meat on Fridays. Bill wasn't Catholic, but he knew we were, and he would come to our house on Fridays with a load of fish he had caught and give it to my folks.

The Yankees offered me a $65,000 bonus. The Giants offered $60,000. The Cardinals still were the highest bidders, but Dickey made me promise I would call him before I signed with any other team and give the Yankees a chance to top the offer.

The Cardinals' strongest pitch to me was that they were in need of a catcher, and I would have the best chance of making the major leagues more quickly with them than I would with the Giants or the Yankees. They pointed out that the Giants had two promising young catchers in Ed Bailey and Tom Haller. The Yankees had Yogi Berra, still a prominent player, and they had Elston Howard coming along. The Cardinals had Hal Smith, an excellent receiver but an impotent bat, and no promising young catchers in their organization.

When the Cardinals made what they said was their final offer of $75,000, they told me to take it or leave it. What did I know? I had no clue. I didn't have an agent. My father was my adviser. So I took their offer and I never made that call to Bill Dickey. I was afraid if I didn't take the Cardinals' offer on the spot, it would be gone. The money was important to me.

I still wonder to this day what would have happened if I had made the call to Dickey. I was embarrassed that I didn't keep my promise to him, but he understood and we remained fast friends until his death.

How would my life have changed if I had made that telephone call to Bill Dickey? I know this: The first game I ever played in Yankee Stadium was Game 1 of the 1964 World Series. I had been in the big leagues for parts of five seasons by then, but I was still intimidated by Yankee Stadium, by New York, by the fans and the media. Maybe I would have been too intimidated to be a success with the Yankees.

As I look back, I have no regrets. As a Cardinal, I got to play in three World Series, twice on the winning side. I played on some great teams, and I am proud to have been associated with some great players. Those Cardinals teams of the sixties not only had talent, they also had some of the brightest people I've ever been around, such as Bob Gibson, Lou Brock, Curt Flood, Joe Torre, Ted Simmons, Dal Maxvill, Mike Shannon, Roger Maris, Orlando Cepeda—guys who would sit around and talk baseball for hours.

You'll notice that my all-time Cardinals team includes many of those players with whom I played. I guess it's natural to give the benefit of the doubt to one's peers. So if my team is a little too heavy with players from the sixties and seventies, please forgive my bias.

I have been a baseball fan since the forties. I was a Cardinal for all or part of 13 seasons, and my job as a baseball broadcaster for Fox takes me to St. Louis frequently. And I must say that baseball in St. Louis is special.

Some of the players on my all-time Cardinals team I never saw play, but I have heard enough about people like Rogers Hornsby, Dizzy Dean, Jim Bottomley, Chick Hafey, and Pepper Martin, and through research, I know they belong on any all-Cardinals team. And I have seen enough of Bob Gibson, Ken Boyer, Ted Simmons, Ozzie Smith, and Mark McGwire to know they also deserve a place on my team.

—TIM MCCARVER
Sarasota, Florida

ONE

Catcher

I THINK I'M SAFE IN SAYING I was part of the most important trade in baseball history. I don't say this out of vanity, although getting traded, especially the first time, is a trauma that hits an athlete personally and with a profound impact.

The reason this trade between the St. Louis Cardinals and the Philadelphia Phillies on October 7, 1969, was so historic is that one of the players traded was Curt Flood, who had been a standout center fielder for the Cardinals for 12 seasons. This was the trade that opened the eyes of the baseball world to the primitive nature of baseball's sanctified reserve clause and set in motion the whole concept of free agency.

Flood refused to report to Philadelphia and though he lost his case in the Supreme Court, a year later the Players Association ultimately won in binding arbitration its contention that players

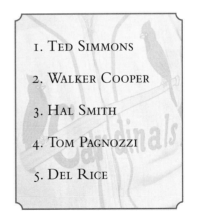

1. TED SIMMONS

2. WALKER COOPER

3. HAL SMITH

4. TOM PAGNOZZI

5. DEL RICE

should not be confined to one team in perpetuity. And, perhaps because of that courageous stand, 31 years later, Alex Rodriguez was able to sign with the Texas Rangers for more than $250 million for 10 years.

*F*ew major league catchers ever get to put down fingers for one Hall of Fame pitcher. Tim McCarver was doubly rewarded. He got to put his fingers down as the primary catcher for two Hall of Fame pitchers, Bob Gibson in St. Louis and Steve Carlton in St. Louis and Philadelphia (McCarver also caught, albeit briefly, Hall of Famers Juan Marichal and Jim Bunning).

It was because of a previous relationship with Carlton that McCarver was able to extend his career and become a rare four-decade major leaguer (1959–1980). In 1975, when he signed on for a second tour of duty with the Phillies, McCarver had already enjoyed one successful major league career with the Cardinals (10 seasons, during which he was the catcher for three National League pennant winners and two World Series champions).

"Timmy had been released by the Red Sox in the middle of the 1975 season," Carlton recalled. "He was on his way back to Memphis, and he stopped off in Philadelphia and met with Paul Owens [general manager of the Phillies], looking for a job as a broadcaster. Owens asked him if he would be interested in playing, instead, and that's how we got together again."

It was a reunion that would benefit both men. McCarver extended his career and added to his baseball lore, and Carlton had two of his greatest years with McCarver as his "personal catcher."

"Bob Boone was our catcher at the time," Carlton said. "No knock on Boonie, who became a tremendous catcher, but we never were in synch. I'd shake him off four or five times before he'd finally ask for the pitch I wanted to throw. With Timmy it was different. We worked real well together. If I shook him off, his next sign was exactly what I was thinking."

It's great to be young and a Cardinal, as I found out before my 18th birthday. *Lew Portnoy, Spectra-Action, Inc.*

The interaction between pitcher and catcher is like any good relationship. When two people are particularly close, often one person in the relationship will say exactly what the other is thinking. It's the same with pitcher and catcher.

"Tim had an uncanny way with pitchers," Carlton said. "Not just me. Dick Ruthven liked pitching to him. A lot of catchers are just putting down fingers. Not Tim. He was always thinking. Tim's a great bridge player, and that's a game where you have to remember what cards have been played. Tim brought that ability to the field as a catcher. He remembered the sequences of pitches we used to get a hitter out. He had great instincts.

"There was a synchronicity between us. He was uncanny. He has such a good mind, and he was a great strategist. We might go through the first two or three innings using just one pitch, instead of showing the other team my whole repertoire in the first two innings. And we wouldn't change until somebody told us to change by the way he swung. I always thought Tim would have made a good manager, but I guess he's better off as a broadcaster. He's had a longer career as a broadcaster than he would have had as a manager.

"When I was with the Cardinals, there were three very funny guys on the team, Bob Uecker, Tim, and Ray Sadecki. Three comedians. They were talking all the time, doing lines. It's not surprising to me that Uecker and McCarver became broadcasters. What's surprising is that Sadecki didn't."

I'll discuss Flood, his extraordinary stand, and his place in baseball history in the chapter dealing with center fielders. For now, back to this trade. I was packaged by the Cardinals with Flood, left-handed reliever Joe Hoerner, and outfielder Byron Browne and dealt to the Phillies in exchange for the great Dick Allen, veteran infielder Cookie Rojas, and a right-handed pitcher, Jerry Johnson.

As I said, the trade hit me hard, since I had signed with the Cardinals, and had played in St. Louis for 10 seasons. The Cardinals were the only organization I knew.

There were several reasons, I believe, for the Cardinals trading me after I had come off a decent year in which I caught 136 games, and more important, had played in three World Series before my 28th birthday.

One reason for the trade, I'm convinced, is that I had begun to get active with the Players' Association. I was the Cardinals' player representative, and I had a few run-ins with the brewery that owned the team (Anheuser-Busch) over things like players getting paid for appearances. I was stirring the waters. The Cardinals are a very close-knit organization and very conservative, and they didn't like having players around who caused turbulence, so I'm sure that's one reason they got rid of me.

"In 1973, I swear Simmons hit 400 balls right on the screws. It seemed everything he hit was a line drive, even his outs."

Another reason was that they had a young catcher coming through their system who they thought was going to be a star, and they wanted to make room for him. The catcher's name was **Ted Simmons**. He was a "can't miss" prospect, a switch-hitter and, man, could he hit.

The first time I can remember seeing Simmons was when he came up to the Cardinals at the end of the 1969 season. He got into five games, had 14 at bats, and three hits, including a game-winning hit. The Cardinals were convinced he was ready to take over the catching job, so while my union activities might have been a reason for the Cardinals trading me, Simmons was the main reason for the trade.

Teddy took over as the Cards' regular catcher in 1970 and almost immediately began showing the promise the Cardinals saw in him by batting over .300 in 1971 and 1972. When I returned to St. Louis in 1973 I saw firsthand what a terrific hitter he was.

Defensively, he wasn't a great technician, but he was very intelligent and a good handler of pitchers. It was his bat that set him apart. In 1973, I swear Simmons hit 400 balls right on the screws. It seemed everything he hit was a line drive, even his outs. He had 619 at-bats and 192 hits, and he batted .310, but I believe with luck, he could have had 300 hits that year. That's how hard he hit the ball all year.

At the end of the 1969 season, one of the writers traveling with the Cardinals wrote an article criticizing my dress and hairstyle. Maybe he was talked into writing the article by Cardinals management to justify getting rid of me. The article wondered whatever happened to that crew cut kid who came up to the Cardinals at the age of 17. Well, times and styles were changing in the sixties. The Vietnam War had changed a nation. We were wearing Nehru jackets and wearing our hair longer. On a dare from Dal Maxvill I had grown long sideburns promoting the style of the day. The article pointed out all of

Ted Simmons, "Simba," who replaced me as catcher for the Cardinals and is number one on my list, is one of the physically toughest human beings I have known. *Lew Portnoy, Spectra-Action, Inc.*

this as an indication that I had changed and was becoming somewhat rebellious.

When Simmons reported to spring training in 1970, he had his hair in a ponytail. It was so long, he needed a rubber band to bind it. I couldn't resist seeking out the writer who had written the article about me, Neal Russo of the *St. Louis Post-Dispatch*, and telling him, "If you can hit, you can wear your hair down to the ground. And you should know that!"

No knock on Teddy's mane—we called him "Simba," which means "lion" in Swahili—for whom I have the greatest respect. He was a very bright guy. Still is. The Pirates made him their general manager. He played at 5′11″, 193 pounds, but he was one of the physically toughest human beings I've ever known. But he never flaunted his strength.

Simmons played 21 seasons in the major leagues, 13 with the Cardinals, five with the Brewers, and three with the Braves. He finished with 2,472 hits,

248 home runs, 1,389 RBIs, and a lifetime average of .285. He caught more games than any catcher in Cardinals history and is in their top ten in at-bats, hits, total bases, doubles, home runs, RBIs, and walks. That's why he's number one on my list of Cardinals catchers and, in my view, the catcher on the all-time switch-hitters team.

I met **Walker Cooper** (my old teammate Don Blasingame married his daughter), but I never saw him play. I have heard enough about him, though, and I am impressed enough by his record to make him number two on my list of all-time Cardinals catchers. Walker was a big bear of a man out of Atherton, Missouri, 6'3", 210 pounds, and a strong hitter in the Ernie Lombardi mold, meaning he couldn't run, but he always hit the ball hard.

He was the catcher on those great Cardinals teams of the forties that won three National League pennants and two World Series in three years, 1942–43–44, and might have won more if World War II hadn't come along. Walker and his brother, Mort, formed what may be the greatest brother battery in baseball history, although there aren't many of them. I can think of Rick and Wes Ferrell, Larry and Norm Sherry, Bobby and Wilmer Shantz.

Big Coop, as he was called, batted .318 with the Cardinals in 1943 and .317 in 1944. He had his biggest year with the Giants in 1947, when he teamed with another ex-Cardinal, Johnny Mize, and helped the Giants set the then National League record for home runs with 221. Cooper batted .305 that season, was fourth in the league with 35 home runs, and was third with 122 RBIs.

Third on my list is **Hal Smith**, who preceded me as the Cardinals' regular catcher. Hal probably would have delayed my promotion to the major leagues, but he suffered a heart attack in 1961 and that accelerated my career and helped me become the Cards' regular catcher in 1963, at the age of 21.

I should point out that there were two Hal Smiths who were contemporaries in the major leagues, both catchers. The other Hal Smith played with five teams, Baltimore, Kansas City, Pittsburgh, Houston, and Cincinnati, and gained a measure of fame with the Pirates in the 1960 World Series against the Yankees. He hit the three-run homer in the bottom of the eighth inning of the seventh game that enabled the Pirates to take the lead. Then, after the Yankees tied the game, they won it in the bottom of the ninth on Bill

My number two Cardinals catcher, Walker Cooper (left), and my number three, Hal Smith (right), were teammates with the Cardinals in 1956. The man in the middle is Clair Troxell, a minor leaguer who never made the big club. My promotion to the Cardinals was accelerated when Smith suffered a heart attack in 1961 and I replaced him. He was known for his soft, pliable hands and could throw lasers. *Bettman/CORBIS*

Mazeroski's sudden-death home run, one of the most famous home runs in baseball history.

That wasn't our Hal Smith. Our Hal Smith hit only 23 home runs in a major league career that spanned 570 games. He drove in only 172 runs and had a lifetime batting average of .258. That may raise some eyebrows among

Tom Pagnozzi, my number four Cardinals catcher, didn't do anything great; he did *everything* very well. *AP/Wide World Photos*

people who might wonder how I could put someone with those offensive numbers third on the Cardinals' all-time list of catchers. The reason is, as a catcher myself, I have a great appreciation of the defensive skills required in the job, and behind the plate Hal was as good as they come. He could catch. He could really catch, with soft, pliable hands, and he could throw lasers. He was a lot like Jerry Grote of the Mets, who was the best defensive catcher I ever saw. Hal Smith was on a par with Grote, and the pitchers loved to pitch to him. Not enough is made, I don't believe, about what a catcher does for a pitcher. All pitchers loved Hal Smith.

Tom Pagnozzi, fourth on my list, was a lot like an umpire. A good umpire is one you hardly notice is on the field. Pagnozzi wasn't great at any one thing, but he was good at a lot of things. A decent hitter and a good receiver, Pagnozzi was good enough to spend 12 seasons with the Cardinals, most of them as their number one catcher. And good enough to have caught 827 games for the Cards, just behind me in fourth place on their all-time list.

Del Rice is fifth on my list. He was an excellent receiver and thrower who had a little pop in his bat and was capable enough to spend 17 years in the major leagues, 11 of them with the Cardinals. But he was miscast. He should have been a cowboy actor. He was tall and rugged, Jack Palance with an Alan Ladd face. The original Marlboro Man. He reminded me of Gary Cooper or Randolph Scott, with his weather-beaten face and rugged good looks. Later, he became a manager for the Angels and a major league scout. I'd run into him often and he was a joy to be around.

We were teammates briefly in 1960. Del was 37 years old and at the end of his career. I was just 18 and had come up to the Cardinals late in the season. Del taught me a valuable lesson that I never forgot. We came out of a meeting one day and Del sat me down and said, "I saw you in there and you looked like you didn't agree with some things. My opinion about meetings is you should sit there, nod your head, and then go out and do what your gut tells you to do. Solly Hemus [our manager] never caught. Johnny Keane never caught. They've never been behind the plate. They haven't seen what you've seen. They don't know what you know. So, just listen to what they say, then go do what you think is right."

It was a credo, learned from Del Rice, that I used throughout my career.

I would be remiss if I didn't include in a discussion of Cardinals catchers one Bill DeLancey. He doesn't make my list of all-time Cardinals catchers, nor should he. He was a Cardinal for only parts of four seasons.

I mention DeLancey because when I first came up, one of the veteran writers told me I reminded him of Bill DeLancey. The reason, I guess, is that we were about the same size—DeLancey 5′11″, 185 pounds, me 6′, 183 pounds—and we were both left-handed-hitting catchers.

One day this writer asked me, "Son, how does it feel to be compared to Bill DeLancey?" I just looked at him with a blank stare. I had no idea who he was talking about.

Later, I looked up DeLancey in the Baseball Encyclopedia and no wonder I didn't know anything about him. He played his last season with the

I learned a lot from teammate Del Rice (right) when I joined the Cardinals at 18 and Del was a 37-year-old veteran catcher. *Bettman/CORBIS*

Cardinals in 1940, the year before I was born. And he died in 1946, when I was five years old. And he was hardly a prominent player.

I mean no disrespect to Bill DeLancey. I have the utmost respect for anyone who makes it to the big leagues. I know how difficult it is to get there, especially for a catcher, the most demanding position on the field. I'm sure the writer who compared me to Bill DeLancey meant it as a compliment. But am I supposed to be flattered being compared to someone who caught only 180 major league games, a little more than one full season?

Statistical Summaries

All statistics are for player's Cardinals career only.

HITTING

G = Games

H = Hits

HR = Home runs

RBI = Runs batted in

SB = Stolen bases

BA = Batting average

Catcher	Years	G	H	HR	RBI	SB	BA
Ted Simmons *Holds team record for most career home runs by a switch-hitter*	1968–80	1,564	1,704	172	929	11	.298
Walker Cooper *Finished second to Musial in 1943 MVP voting*	1940–45 1956–57	525	493	25	265	11	.296
Hal Smith *All-Star selection in 1957 and 1959*	1956–61	566	437	23	172	6	.258

(continued)	Years	G	H	HR	RBI	SB	BA
Tom Pagnozzi *First Cardinal catcher to win Gold Glove, in 1991 (also won in 1992 and 1994)*	1987–98	927	733	44	320	18	.253
Del Rice *Career high 147 games caught in 1952*	1945–55 1960	1,038	756	60	323	2	.241

FIELDING

PO = Put-outs

A = Assists

E = Errors

DP = Double plays

TC/G = Total chances divided by games played

FA = Fielding average

Catcher	PO	A	E	DP	TC/G	FA
Ted Simmons	7,460	755	104	87	5.8	.987
Walker Cooper	1,876	204	56	29	5.0	.974
Hal Smith	2,797	247	33	43	5.7	.989
Tom Pagnozzi	4,124	389	38	47	5.5	.992
Del Rice	4,307	455	59	63	4.7	.988

TWO

First Baseman

WHEN I HEARD THAT **Mark McGwire** had decided to retire, I was dumbfounded. I was disappointed and confused. This was October of 2001, and I wondered why Mark wouldn't announce his retirement during the World Series. But vintage McGwire reared his humble head once more.

Baseball would have brought Mark to the World Series and had him make his announcement on a national stage; or at least they would have brought him to New York where he could state to the national media his intention to leave baseball. This would have been done had Commissioner Bud Selig and baseball's hierarchy known of McGwire's surprising plans. They didn't; thus, McGwire's retirement came as a strange footnote after a staggering World Series that thrust baseball back into the nation's consciousness.

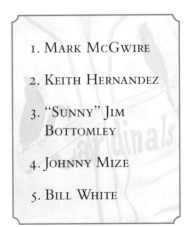

1. MARK MCGWIRE

2. KEITH HERNANDEZ

3. "SUNNY" JIM BOTTOMLEY

4. JOHNNY MIZE

5. BILL WHITE

This odd announcement was in stark contrast to just three years earlier when McGwire captured the imagination of a nation by hitting 70 home runs, bringing hundreds of thousands of fans out to ballparks all across the country and creating countless numbers of new fans.

If Babe Ruth had announced his retirement similarly in 1930, three years after setting a new home-run record, would that announcement have been dismissed in such a somber fashion? McGwire's 70 home runs at least matched the enormity of Ruth's 60 home runs 71 years earlier. That's how big Mark McGwire was—as big as Babe Ruth was in his day. That's how monumental his achievement was in 1998. It was Ruthian. Or, put another way, Ruth's achievement was McGwirean.

"I don't think what Mark did was fully appreciated because he spoiled people."

But, then, grandstanding, posturing, and bravado never have been what Mark McGwire is about. He was the game's biggest star, but he never was its highest paid player. Not that McGwire was deprived. He made $15 million a year, but he could have demanded more, and the Cardinals would have had to pay him. They could have paid him much, much more, and still he would have been a bargain. He was satisfied with what he made, and he genuinely put playing in St. Louis above signing for millions more elsewhere.

The Cardinals have had a few great first basemen, and McGwire was a Cardinal for only four-and-a-half seasons, but he belongs on the top of the list by the sheer magnitude of his accomplishments. What he did was the stuff of legends. He was the essence of power, one of the great home-run hitters of all time.

I don't think what Mark did was fully appreciated because he spoiled people. In 1998, when he and Sammy Sosa were chasing Roger Maris' home-run record, Mark hit four home runs the last two days of the season. He made it look so easy that some might not have fully appreciated the degree of difficulty of hitting 70 home runs. Even today, when home runs are more plentiful than ever, his feat will endure as one of the greatest in the history of American sports.

The same goes for Barry Bonds. What Bonds did in 2001, hitting 73 home runs, was truly electrifying. Add to that an all-time record for slugging average at .863, an all-time record for walks with 177, which he broke the following season, a .515 on-base percentage, and a .328 batting average, all at the age of 37. It's mind-boggling.

The only other player to have a slugging average higher than .800, an on-base percentage higher than .500, more than 150 walks, and more than 50 home runs in the same season was Babe Ruth. And he did that 80 years before Bonds did.

Think of it. Bonds had 476 official at-bats in 2001, not counting walks, sacrifice flies, and hit-by-pitches, and hit 73 home runs. That's one home run for every six-and-a-half at-bats. Unbelievable! In 1927, when he hit 60 home runs, Ruth had one home run for every nine at-bats. McGwire, when he hit 70 homers in 1998, had one for every 7.3 at-bats. Bobby Valentine has said, and I agree, that you can make a case that in 2001, Barry Bonds had the greatest offensive season in the history of baseball.

The Cardinals had many great first basemen, but how could I not put Mark McGwire on the top of my list? Although he was a Cardinal for only 4½ seasons, his record-breaking 70 home runs in 1998 is one of the great accomplishments in baseball history and is not diminished one bit by the fact that Barry Bonds broke that record three years later.
AP/Wide World Photos

Bonds stands alone with his 73 home runs, but people took that for granted because it came only three years after McGwire broke the record. Don't forget, McGwire broke Maris' record 37 years after Maris broke Babe Ruth's record. And Ruth's record lasted 34 years before Maris broke it.

The fact that Bonds broke the record only three years after McGwire set it does not diminish what Bonds did. It points more to the achievement of Bonds. Just as McGwire's breaking Maris' record does not diminish what Maris did, and Maris' breaking Ruth's record does not diminish what Ruth did.

"I saw Vic Power. I saw Wes Parker, Ron Fairly, Don Mattingly, and J. T. Snow. They all were outstanding defensive first basemen. Hernandez was better. No contest."

What McGwire did was awesome. In four years, from 1996 to 1999, he averaged 61 home runs a year. Until Mark came along, only one player in the history of baseball had ever hit 61 home runs in one year.

At 6′5″, 250 pounds, McGwire exuded power. He had this royal bearing at the plate. Even his retirement announcement was regal. Low-key and humble. No big fanfare. It wasn't like him to call attention to himself, make himself out to be bigger than the game. Although I was disappointed at his bowing out in such stealthy understatement, the more I thought about it, the more I understood it. It wasn't his style to overshadow anybody else.

18

What McGwire was with a bat in his hands, **Keith Hernandez** was with a glove in his. His defense parallels McGwire's offense, and that's not overstatement or hyperbole. Keith was simply the best. Even with all his home runs, McGwire never won the Most Valuable Player award. Hernandez did. In 1979 he shared the award with Willie Stargell, the only time in baseball history when two players have shared MVP honors.

I saw Vic Power. I saw Wes Parker, Ron Fairly, Don Mattingly, and J. T. Snow. They all were outstanding defensive first basemen. Hernandez was better. No contest.

In the old days, teams would stick guys on first base who couldn't play anywhere else. They usually were big, lumbering men who could hit, and in the days before the designated hitter, managers, just to get their bats in the lineup, would put those types on first base where it was believed they would do the least damage.

What Mark McGwire was to offense, Keith Hernandez was to defense: the best fielding first baseman I have ever seen. *Lew Portnoy, Spectra-Action, Inc.*

Then along came people like Fairly, Parker, and Keith Hernandez, who opened the eyes of baseball people to the importance of first base as a defensive position.

Hernandez, number two on my team, may be the best defensive first baseman ever. He did things no first baseman ever did. The Mets used him as a cut-off man on balls hit down the right-field line. A first baseman as a cut-off man! That was unheard of.

As far as throwing and bunt coverage, he gave a new dimension to playing the position. And he was an intelligent player. He knew pitching and pitchers. He often played the pitcher, not the hitter. With the Mets, Hernandez would position himself depending on who was pitching. For example, he knew left-handed hitters weren't going to pull the ball against Doc Gooden or Sid Fernandez, so Keith would play off the bag.

You'd look at Keith's defensive position and you'd say to yourself, "My God, look at this. Look how far he's playing in the hole." The Mets had a second baseman, Wally Backman, who had no range to his right. He didn't have to have range to his right because he was allowed to plug his deficiency by playing close to second base. Hernandez was there to suck up balls in the hole on the right side.

I've heard people talk about how great a first baseman Gil Hodges was, and I have no doubt he was. So was Vic Power. I saw him, and he played the position with panache. But they were right-handed throwers and they couldn't do the things a left-handed thrower, like Hernandez, could. How could whoever invented baseball, Alexander Cartwright or Abner Doubleday, know that first base was a left-hander's position?

With all his greatness defensively, the thing that really set Hernandez apart was the way he covered bunts. It's remarkable to me that a guy who couldn't run was so quick and agile. He had marvelous instincts and reflexes, and despite his lack of speed, his first step was lightning fast.

For example, in a bunt situation with runners on first and second, Keith would cheat toward the mound, knowing the hitter's intention was to bunt down the third-base line so that the third baseman would field it, thereby leaving third base uncovered. Hernandez was so quick, he often fielded that bunt down the third-base line, the third baseman would anchor at his position, and Keith would throw the lead runner out. Often, Hernandez would end up in foul territory between home and third. I saw him do it more than a handful of times and it never failed to amaze me.

Third and fourth on my list are **"Sunny" Jim Bottomley** and **Johnny Mize**. I never saw either of them play, but you can't ignore their records. Both are in the Hall of Fame.

Bottomley played for the Cardinals in the twenties and thirties and led the National League in triples, home runs, and RBIs in 1928. It isn't often a guy

Between them, Ripper Collins (left) and "Sunny" Jim Bottomley manned first base for the Cardinals for 14 years, 1923 to 1936. Each led the National League in home runs and, combined, they had eight seasons with 100 or more runs batted in—two for Collins, six for Bottomley. *AP/Wide World Photos*

Johnny Mize, the "Big Cat," was a lumbering first baseman, one of the National League's premier home-run hitters with the Giants, and a pinch-hitter par excellence with the Yankees. Early in his career (when he was with the Cardinals) he led the league in triples (16) in 1938 and in batting (.349) in 1939. *AP/Wide World Photos*

leads the league in triples and home runs in the same year, a rare combination of power and speed.

Bottomley batted over .300 nine times in his 11 seasons with the Cardinals, including .371 in 1923 (Rogers Hornsby led the league that year at .384) and .367 in 1925 (again, his teammate Hornsby beat Bottomley out of the batting title by hitting .403). Bottomley also drove in more than 100 runs six times with the Cardinals. In 16 major league seasons (three with Cincinnati, two with the St. Louis Browns), he had a lifetime average of .310.

Johnny Mize was typical of those lumbering first basemen I talked about earlier. He was from Decatur, Georgia, 6′2″ tall, and he is listed at 215 pounds, but in the films I've seen of him, he looked to be more like 240 or 250.

They called him the "Big Cat," but from what I've heard, he was hardly catlike as a first baseman. He had good hands, but no range.

As a hitter, Mize was something else. He and Ralph Kiner were the premier power hitters of their day, in the forties. Mize led the league in home runs four times and belted 51 for the New York Giants in 1947, when 50 home runs was a rarity in baseball.

*B*aseball's two premier power hitters of the forties were Ralph Kiner and Johnny Mize, the "Big Cat." They were the Mark McGwire and Sammy Sosa of their day.

Mize began his career with the Cardinals and in six seasons in St. Louis won a National League batting title and two home-run championships. He was at the peak of his career when the Cardinals traded him in 1942 to the New York Giants for three journeyman players and, for the penurious Cardinals the most important part of the deal, $50,000.

In New York, Mize teamed with Mel Ott to form a potent home-run tandem. In 1942, Ott and Mize finished 1-2 in the National League in home runs. After the season, Mize spent three years in the United States Navy. When he returned in 1946, there was a new home-run slugger in the National League, Pirates rookie Ralph Kiner, and the two battled to the wire for the league home-run championship, with Kiner topping Mize by one, 23–22. In each of the next two years, Kiner and Mize tied for the National League home-run title.

Until 1947, only four men had hit 50 home runs in a season. Babe Ruth did it three times, Jimmie Foxx twice, Hank Greenberg and Hack Wilson once each. In 1947, both Kiner and Mize joined the exclusive 50-homer club, each with 51. They tied again in 1948 with 40 each.

Kiner, a member of the Hall of Fame, tied for or won the National League home-run championship for seven consecutive years, from 1946 to 1952. He has been a broadcaster for the New York Mets since their inception in 1962.

"He was my broadcast partner for 16 memorable years," said Tim McCarver. "During that time I came to understand why everyone loves Ralph."

Kiner remembers Mize, his home-run rival, fondly.

"Mize was a great, great hitter," Kiner said. "In my book, you have to put him up there with the great hitters of all time, not only as a power hitter but as a contact hitter as well. The amazing thing about him is that he was a tough guy to strike out [only 524 strikeouts and 359 home runs in his career, 42 strikeouts and 51 homers in 1947].

"The hitter Mize most reminded me of is Stan Musial. I think of him and Musial alike, great average hitters who used the whole field. It wasn't until he was traded to the Giants that Mize changed his style of hitting. The Polo Grounds had this huge center field, more than 450 feet away, and the power alleys were deep. But it was only 258 feet down the right-field line, so Mize waited on the ball and became a pull hitter and a big home-run threat.

"Mize was very good with the glove. He was no Keith Hernandez. He wasn't fast, but he had great hands.

Another rarity is that for a guy who couldn't run a lick, Mize put up some impressive batting averages. In 1937 he finished second in the batting race to another Cardinal, Joe Medwick, who won the triple crown. That was the last time it was done in the National League. Two seasons later, Mize won the batting title. In 13 seasons with the Cardinals, the Giants, and the Yankees (for whom he was a pinch-hitter par excellence), Mize had a lifetime batting average of .312.

For number five on my all-time list of Cardinals first basemen, I have to get personal. My teammate **Bill White** was the leader of the Cardinals of the sixties, a gentleman and a man of great intelligence who had the respect of everybody, especially his teammates. He eventually became president of the National League.

Bill and Ken Boyer were the big run producers for the Cardinals teams of the early sixties. Bill batted over .300, hit more than 20 home runs, and drove in more than 100 runs for three consecutive seasons, 1962, 1963, and 1964.

Bill doesn't get the credit he deserves as a defensive player, but he was a superb first baseman who could do everything but throw. He had soft hands for a big man and was excellent at the first-short-first double play, the 3-6-3. Like Hernandez, he couldn't run, but he had great instincts and reflexes and a quick first two steps.

I would be remiss if I didn't make mention here of Orlando Cepeda, "Cha-Cha." He doesn't make my top five because he played only two-and-a-half seasons with the Cardinals. But those two-plus years were extraordinary, particularly 1967, when he batted .325, hit 25 homers, led the league with 111

Bill White was intelligent, a fierce competitor, a leader, and a run producer for the Cardinals in the sixties. He batted over .300, had more than 20 home runs, and drove in more than 100 runs for three consecutive seasons, 1962–1964. He later became president of the National League. *Bettman/CORBIS*

runs batted in, and was the National League's unanimous Most Valuable Player.

Another first baseman who gets overlooked is Jim "Ripper" Collins, who managed Ralph Kiner in the minor leagues. He was only 5′9″ tall, small for a first baseman, but he was the top slugger for the Gashouse Gang. He led the National League in home runs in 1934 with 35. That stood as the league record for home runs by a switch hitter until Howard Johnson of the Mets broke it 53 years later.

ourteen years after Jackie Robinson broke baseball's color line, two years after the last major league team, the Boston Red Sox, became integrated, black players were still housed in separate quarters during spring training.

"We lived in private houses, with African-American families," said Bob Gibson, whose first major league training camp was in 1958 with the Cardinals in St. Petersburg.

Although they were the southernmost city in the major leagues at the time, the Cardinals were not the last to integrate, and they were the first to house all their players under the same roof in spring training. Tom Alston, a first baseman from Greensboro, North Carolina, and Brooks Lawrence, a right-handed pitcher from Springfield, Ohio, were the first black players to join the Cardinals, in 1954. "Toothpick" Sam Jones came along in 1957, Curt Flood in 1958, and Gibson, George Crowe, and Bill White in 1959.

White had come to the major leagues in 1956 with the New York Giants and moved with them to San Francisco. Finding themselves with a plethora of outstanding first-base prospects (Orlando Cepeda was already in San Francisco; Willie McCovey was on the way), the Giants traded White to the Cardinals in March of 1959. With Stan Musial entrenched at first base in St. Louis and the Cardinals eager to get White's productive bat in the lineup, they tried him in the outfield. They even played him in center field, although they had one of the best in the game in Curt Flood.

"I was the worst center fielder in the history of the game, " said White. "I couldn't run, I couldn't throw, and I wasn't very good on fly balls."

Eventually, the Cardinals moved Musial to left field, put Flood in center field, where he belonged, and moved White to his natural position, first base, where he became one of the best of his time at that position, a consistent .300 hitter, a 20- to 25-home-run hitter, a 100 RBI man, and a mainstay of the 1964 world championship team.

In the spring of 1961, three years before the Civil Rights Act, the Cardinals purchased the Sheraton Outrigger Hotel in St. Petersburg, and it became the team's official spring-training headquarters and residence for all players without regard to color. As a show of unity, all Cardinals players lived in the hotel during spring training. Even Stan Musial, the greatest Cardinal of them all, left his home on St. Petersburg Beach and moved his family into the Outrigger.

The Cardinals' decision was not entirely altruistic, however. Executives of the Anheuser-Busch Brewery, owner of the team, were fearful of a boycott of their product by blacks, and integrated quarters for the Cardinals in spring training was largely a business decision.

According to Bob Gibson, "The move that led to the Cardinals buying the hotel where we would all live together in spring training was spearheaded by Bill White." But White, among the most cerebral and socially conscious baseball players, minimizes his role.

"It was [Cardinals general manager] Bing Devine," said White. "He was the catalyst in the things that were done in St. Petersburg and throughout Florida. He believed it would be best for all concerned if we all lived together."

Statistical Summaries

All statistics are for player's Cardinals career only.

HITTING

G = Games

H = Hits

HR = Home runs

RBI = Runs batted in

SB = Stolen bases

BA = Batting average

First Baseman	Years	G	H	HR	RBI	SB	BA
Mark McGwire *Sixty percent of his hits went for extra bases in 1998*	1997–2001	545	469	220	473	4	.270
Keith Hernandez *Played in 150 games or more during nine different seasons in his career*	1974–83	1,165	1,217	81	595	81	.299
Jim Bottomley *One of only five players with 20 or more 2B, 3B, and HR in a season (1928)*	1922–32	1,392	1,727	181	1,105	50	.325

(continued)	Years	G	H	HR	RBI	SB	BA
Johnny Mize *Led N.L. in 2B, 3B, HR, RBI, BA, SA in a season while with Cards*	1936–41	854	1,048	158	653	14	.336
Bill White *Drove in a run in 10 consecutive games in 1961*	1959–65 1969	1,113	1,241	140	631	65	.298

FIELDING

PO = Put-outs

A = Assists

E = Errors

DP = Double plays

TC/G = Total chances divided by games played

FA = Fielding average

First Baseman	PO	A	E	DP	TC/G	FA
Mark McGwire	4,166	267	31	396	8.7	.993
Keith Hernandez	10,572	879	73	991	10.3	.994
Jim Bottomley	13,160	553	174	1,151	10.4	.987
Johnny Mize	7,383	478	79	616	9.8	.990
Bill White	8,283	610	69	752	9.2	.992

THREE

Second Baseman

Iт's ironic that the number one and number three second basemen on my all-time Cardinals list were traded for each other after the 1926 season in one of the most highly publicized and hotly debated trades in baseball history. **Rogers Hornsby** and **Frankie Frisch**, two future Hall of Famers, traded for one another. To put it in a modern context, it would be like the Yankees trading Derek Jeter to Texas for Alex Rodriguez. I'll get to Frisch in a moment. First, let's talk about my number one pick, Hornsby.

There were, of course, extenuating circumstances to that controversial trade, not the least of which was Hornsby's irascible personality and his demands for more money from the Cardinals. Through the years, I have talked with many people who knew Rogers Hornsby. The legendary, cantankerous, bombastic, redoubtable, contentious Hornsby. Nobody had a nice word to say about him.

1. Rogers Hornsby

2. Red Schoendienst

3. Frankie Frisch

4. Julian Javier

5. Tommy Herr

Hornsby blasted Roger Maris publicly after Maris broke Babe Ruth's home-run record in 1961. Maris came to the Cardinals in 1967, and we became good friends. He was a man of even disposition, but if you wanted to raise his ire, all you had to do was mention the name Rogers Hornsby.

Hornsby was a sour and bitter man, not only in later life, but apparently throughout his life. But as a hitter, he was incredible. He has been called "the greatest right-handed hitter in baseball history," and when people select an all-time team, Hornsby invariably gets the nod at second base.

"Through the years I have talked with many people who knew Rogers Hornsby—the legendary, cantankerous, bombastic, redoubtable, contentious Hornsby. Nobody had a nice word to say about him."

In 1926, his 12th year with the Cardinals, Hornsby batted .317, drove in 93 runs, and managed the Cards to their first National League pennant and a World Series victory in seven games over the Yankees of Babe Ruth and Lou Gehrig. In fact, the Cardinals won the seventh game, 3–2, and clinched the Series when Ruth made the final out when he was thrown out attempting to steal second base.

Hornsby's .317 average in 1926 was a sharp decline for a man who had won the National League batting title in each of the six previous years, three times with averages over .400. But his decline was not the reason he was traded. He was still only 30 at the time, and in good health, so there was no reason to believe he wouldn't rebound in 1927 and once again become the dominant hitter in the league.

Hornsby, a defiant man, had no respect for authority and often battled with his owners. He would bar club officials from the clubhouse, telling them to mind their own business and leave him and his players alone to do their jobs. Cardinals owner Sam Breadon had had enough of Hornsby's insubordination, and the final straw came when Hornsby demanded a three-year contract at $50,000 per year. Breadon, not regarded as the most munificent of owners, countered with an offer of one year. When the dispute reached a stalemate, Breadon sought a solution and found it by trading Hornsby to the Giants for another all-star second baseman—Frisch—and pitcher Jimmy Ring.

At the time, the trade was greeted with a storm of protest from Cardinals fans. I can only imagine how the St. Louis writers reacted to the trade of a Cardinals icon. Eventually, Frisch became a hero in St. Louis, a leader of the Gashouse Gang on the field and in the dugout as manager.

Hornsby bounced back from his relatively poor 1926 season to bat .361 for the Giants in 1927, but they, too, tired quickly of his boorishness and traded him after one year to the Boston Braves. He won the batting title in 1928 when he batted .387 for the Braves, but once again he was traded after one

He was cantankerous, ornery, irascible, bombastic, contentious, and not a nice man, but Rogers Hornsby has been called the greatest right-handed hitter in baseball history by many.
AP/Wide World Photos

season, this time to the Cubs. He would come back to the Cardinals for 46 games in 1933, then move on to the St. Louis Browns as their player/manager.

Hornsby finished up his career as a manager with the Browns and the Cincinnati Reds, never finishing higher than sixth place in eight seasons. He died in Chicago in 1963, a beaten, bitter, and friendless man.

Despite being such an ornery cuss, Hornsby's accomplishments on the baseball field cannot be dismissed lightly. I am of the belief that hitting was a lot easier in the twenties and thirties than it is today. They had no night games back then and no coast-to-coast travel. There were only eight teams in the league, which meant you got to see the same pitchers over and over. And relief pitching had not become prominent, which meant batters were often hitting against tired pitchers.

The game is much more specialized today. You have middle-inning pitchers, set-up men, and closers. There are more teams, so you might not see the same pitcher more than twice a season. And the variety of pitches used today is much more vast than in the old days, when hitters rarely saw sliders and split-fingered fastballs, and pitchers rarely threw 98 and 99 mph fastballs.

Nevertheless, what Rogers Hornsby accomplished is mind-boggling: seven batting titles; a five-year period from 1921 to 1925 in which he averaged over .400; a .424 batting average in 1924, the highest in baseball history; and a career batting average of .358, second to Ty Cobb and just ahead of "Shoeless," but not hitless, Joe Jackson.

Don't get the idea that Hornsby was merely a slap hitter who just put the bat on the ball. He stood only 5'11" and weighed 175 pounds, but he was one of the most feared power hitters of his day. Twice he led the league in homers, with 42 in 1922 and 39 in 1925. Four times he led the league in RBIs, with a high of 152 in 1922.

Part of Hornsby's mystique was his nickname, "Rajah." An Indian prince. Such a regal name for a man who was anything but regal, except as a baseball player.

I met Hornsby when he was a coach for the Mets in 1962. It was not a pleasant experience. He died the following year in Chicago.

We learn as children that you shouldn't speak ill of the dead, but to extol at his death someone who was not a good person does a disservice to the nice people who lived exemplary lives. All people are not the same, and dying didn't make Rogers Hornsby a better person.

Another Hall of Famer makes my list, and here again I'll show my bias by putting **Red Schoendienst** second. It isn't because Red is the gentlest and nicest of men or because he was my manager. He earned the high rating with a lifetime .289 average over 19 seasons; ranking in the Cardinals' top ten in at-bats, runs, hits, total bases, games played, and doubles; and playing marvelous defense.

There's a saying in baseball that you can tell the guys who were good fielders by the way they shake hands. When you shake Red's hand, it's as soft as a pillow, and that's the way he was as a fielder. Soft, pliable, flexible hands.

An infielder is taught to field a ground ball below the hop, to absorb the hop, and Red was a master at that. An example of a second baseman, and a good one, who didn't field the ball below the hop is Ryne Sandberg. He violated all the rules. He was a stabber. He became so good at it; he made

Red Schoendienst made the Hall of Fame as a slick-fielding, switch-hitting second baseman. He also makes my Hall of Fame of nice people. *AP/Wide World Photos*

himself into an outstanding second baseman, however unorthodox. But he never was as smooth a fielder as Schoendienst, who did everything by the book.

Another thing about Red, he had a quick bat. Howard Pollett, the fine left-hander for the Cardinals in the forties, said you couldn't throw a fastball past Red.

Frankie Frisch, third on my list, was known as the "Fordham Flash," which suggests he was a speedster. In fact, Frisch led the league in steals three times, but he never stole 50 bases in any season. When Frisch played in the twenties and thirties, they weren't stealing 100 bases like Maury Wills, Vince Coleman, Lou Brock, and Rickey Henderson did in later years.

In 1931, Frisch became the first National League Most Valuable Player selected under the present system of voting, by a panel made up of members of the Baseball Writers Association of America. That year, he beat out his teammate Chick Hafey, who tied for the batting title with the Giants' Bill Terry at .349, and Chuck Klein of the Phillies, who led the league with 31 home runs and 121 RBIs.

Frisch batted .311, led the league with 28 stolen bases, and was the spark-plug of the famed Gashouse Gang that won the National League pennant by 13 games, then beat the Philadelphia Athletics of Connie Mack in a seven-game World Series.

Frisch played 19 seasons in the major leagues, 11 of them with the Cardinals, and finished his career with a lifetime batting average of .316. He later became a player/manager for the Cardinals and also managed the Pirates and Cubs. He, along with Jack Graney, Waite Hoyt, Dizzy Dean, and Buddy Blattner, was also one of the first players-turned-broadcasters.

The identity of Frisch with the Gashouse Gang always amused me. Fordham is a wonderful institution in New York and is run by the Jesuits, so here you have a college man as a leader on a team that was the antithesis of higher education. Pepper Martin, Dizzy Dean—any connection between that team and education was purely coincidental. Dizzy Dean didn't even know how to spell *Jesuits*.

I warned you that I would be biased when it came to some of my teammates, and my bias may come out more with **Julian Javier** than with any other player. Hoolie was one of the most unappreciated players I've ever been

Frank Frisch was called the "Fordham Flash," but his highest stolen-base total was 49 with the Giants in 1921. He was miscast with the "Gashouse Gang," a college man amidst a bunch of rabble-rousers. It was logical that he would become their manager. *AP/Wide World Photos*

For my money, Julian Javier, shown here scoring against the Mets, was a better second baseman than Hall of Famer Bill Mazeroski. Hoolie was quicker and faster than Maz; check him out here showing his speed while scoring against the Mets. *Bettman/CORBIS*

around. When I say he was unappreciated, I mean by the public and the base-ball fraternity in general, certainly not by his teammates.

You couldn't really appreciate Javier unless you saw him on a day-to-day basis, but any Cardinal who played with him can attest to his greatness as a second baseman.

Javier was one of the early imports from the Dominican Republic. He came from the town of San Francisco de Macoris, which is in the north of the Dominican Republic and is not to be confused with the more well-known San Pedro de Macoris, which is on the southernmost part of the island and has produced more major leaguers per square mile than any other place on Earth. He is the father of Stan Javier, who has had a long and productive major league career and is a fine man, just like his dad. This apple didn't fall far from the tree.

One of the reasons Hoolie never got the credit he deserved is that he didn't have the offensive stats to go along with his defensive brilliance. He had a lifetime batting average of .257, and he hit only 78 home runs and drove in just 506 runs in a 13-year major league career. Unfortunately, with rare exceptions (Ozzie Smith, for example), players are judged more for their offensive contributions than for their defense and all-around play.

Another reason Javier has been overlooked is that his contemporary, Bill Mazeroski of the Pirates, who was regarded as the premier second baseman of his day, overshadowed him. Nothing against Maz, but Javier was better. I admired Maz's defensive talent and his quick hands, but he didn't have Javier's range. Hoolie went back on pop flies almost as well as Roberto Alomar, who, by the way, is the best second baseman I've ever seen.

Mazeroski built his reputation because of his quick hands and his ability to turn the double play. His style was much different from Javier's. Maz just stuck his left leg out like a tree trunk and let the runner slam into his leg. The runner paid a price, and so did Mazeroski. He'd hang in there and take a pounding.

Javier's technique was different. Runners never got to his legs. He was the "Phantom." He reinvented the "neighborhood play" at second (you didn't have to actually touch second base, all you had to do was be in the vicinity of the bag and you'd get the call). Javier was rarely on the bag. His timing was perfect and his hands and feet were so quick, you often couldn't even see the exchange.

39

When I consider Javier's all-around play, I place him fourth on my list. If I were rating players by defense alone, however, Javier would be at the top.

Fifth on my list of all-time Cardinals second basemen is **Tommy Herr**, a leader of Whitey Herzog's roadrunner offense of the eighties. He's 10th on the Cards' all-time list in steals; second in game-winning hits; and fifth in games played by Cardinals' second basemen.

In 1985 Tommy Herr, a leader of Whitey Herzog's roadrunner offense, hit only eight home runs, but still drove in 110 runs. *Lew Portnoy, Spectra-Action, Inc.*

Tommy was a steady ballplayer and a good RBI man who drove in 110 runs in 1985. You know he had to be a good RBI man because he hit only eight home runs that year, so he was not padding his RBI total by getting them in bunches with home runs. He was earning his RBIs by getting big hits with runners in scoring position.

Statistical Summaries

All statistics are for player's Cardinals career only.

HITTING

G = Games

H = Hits

HR = Home runs

RBI = Runs batted in

SB = Stolen bases

BA = Batting average

Second Baseman	Years	G	H	HR	RBI	SB	BA
Rogers Hornsby *Only N.L. player to win two Triple Crowns (1922, 1925)*	1915–26 1933	1,580	2,110	193	1,072	118	.359
Red Schoendienst *Led N.L. in stolen bases as a rookie with 26 in 1945*	1945–56 1961–63	1,795	1,980	65	651	80	.289
Frankie Frisch *Played in more World Series games (50) and had more hits (58) than any other N.L. player*	1927–37	1,311	1,577	51	720	195	.312

(continued)	Years	G	H	HR	RBI	SB	BA
Julian Javier *Hit .360 in 1967 World Series vs. Boston*	1960–71	1,578	1,450	76	494	134	.258
Tommy Herr *Led N.L. second basemen in double plays three times (1981, 1984, 1986)*	1979–88	1,029	1,021	19	435	152	.274

FIELDING

PO = Put-outs

A = Assists

E = Errors

DP = Double plays

TC/G = Total chances divided by games played

FA = Fielding average

Second Baseman	PO	A	E	DP	TC/G	FA
Rogers Hornsby	2,144	3,263	207	554	5.6	.963
Red Schoendienst	3,684	4,130	137	1,092	5.6	.983
Frankie Frisch	2,879	3,807	170	709	6.0	.975
Julian Javier	3,377	4,107	219	907	5.0	.972
Tommy Herr	2,122	2,892	59	730	5.1	.988

FOUR

Shortstop

REMEMBER THE TELEVISION SHOW in the fifties called *Mr. Wizard*? It was a children's show, and Mr. Wizard was a scientist of sorts. He would do experiments and explain things, like how a dam works and stuff like that, practical information in language that children could understand. I found myself absorbed by this show on many an afternoon.

I bring this up because I thought of that television show more than once while I was watching **Ozzie Smith** play shortstop. He was the Mr. Wizard of shortstops, or as he was often called, "The Wizard of Oz."

Without question, Ozzie Smith was one of a kind, in my mind the greatest defensive shortstop who ever played the game. His athletic ability was such that he would come onto the field, run out to his position, and do a back flip. Forget playing the position. Most shortstops couldn't even try to get to

1. OZZIE SMITH

2. MARTY "SLATS" MARION

3. DAL MAXVILL

4. DICK GROAT

5. LEO DUROCHER

their position in that fashion. Fans and players never thought he was a hot dog, and he was never perceived as such. He was synchronized, hand-and-foot coordination extraordinaire.

Ozzie Smith, the "Wizard," was voted into the Hall of Fame strictly for his glove. But what a glove! I believe he was the greatest shortstop in baseball history. You had to see him to appreciate his value to a team. *AP/Wide World Photos*

A lot of infielders dive for a ball with no chance whatsoever of making the play. Ozzie dived and not only came up with the ball, but also got to his feet so quickly from a prone position that he usually got his man. His range was unbelievable. His speed and quickness were electric. How do you dive for a ball, get to your feet, and still throw runners out by more than a step? No shortstop, then or now, did it with such consistency.

Whitey Herzog deserves full credit for recognizing Ozzie's value. Whitey was the Cardinals' manager when they traded Garry Templeton to San Diego for Smith before the 1982 season. It was a trade that didn't make sense in St. Louis at the time because of the talent involved. Garry was a terrific offensive player, one of the finest young talents around at the time, but he was not a fan favorite in St. Louis. He once gave the crowd the finger and grabbed his crotch; he was yanked from the game. Despite his talent, the Cardinals had to get rid of him.

Ozzie, on the other hand, had nowhere near the offensive credentials of Templeton, but he played a position that didn't require that. To prove the point, he became the anchor of an infield that helped the Cardinals win three pennants and one World Series in six years.

Herzog used to say, "I don't care if he doesn't drive in 100 runs a year, he saves more than 100 runs a year with his glove."

The trade from San Diego to St. Louis also meant that Ozzie was going from grass to artificial surface. Not that Ozzie didn't excel on grass; he did. But turf was more conducive to his style of play. It adds a new dimension to playing the infield. Perhaps he would have been just as flashy in San Diego, but the hops are truer on the artificial surface and the ball gets to the infield faster, which makes a strong arm vital. Ozzie had to play deeper in St. Louis than he did in San Diego. Though he never had a strong arm, he could rely on quickness of delivery to get his outs.

The turf allowed him to make those spectacular plays that earned him his reputation for defense. Ozzie was a head-turner, like Bo Derek was a head-turner. If you were at the ballgame with your friend, or your son or daughter, you'd see Ozzie make one of his fantastic plays and it would leave you speechless. You'd turn to your companion and just shake your head. He'd make your eyes pop.

Ozzie was the prototype shortstop. He was molded to his position as Johnny Bench was molded to his. Bench was the prototype catcher. He may have been a Hall of Famer as a left fielder, but he would have been just one of many. As a catcher, he stood apart from everybody else.

That's how it was with Ozzie Smith as a shortstop. Nobody was carved into a position like Ozzie Smith at shortstop. Alex Rodriguez has added a new dimension to shortstops by hitting 50 home runs. There was a time, not too long ago, when you couldn't imagine a shortstop hitting 50 homers. And you could never imagine a shortstop with the defensive skills of Ozzie Smith. He was the quintessential defensive shortstop.

I believe you can say Ozzie Smith is the first player voted into the Hall of Fame strictly for his glove. The venerable Hall, for once, forgot about numbers for numbers' sake and understood what Herzog understood—saving runs was at least as important as driving them in.

When he first came up, Ozzie was the All-American out. You could knock the bat out of his hands. Pitchers would try to make him lift the ball in the air because he wasn't big and strong enough to hit it out of the park. Ozzie made himself into a good hitter with hard work, discipline, and intelligence. He learned to take advantage of the artificial surface and his speed. Some guys learn how to hit. Others learn how to hit by taking pitches they can't hit. Ozzie disciplined himself to lay off the high strike and force pitchers to get the ball down in the strike zone, and he put the ball in play on the ground. He would drive the ball through the infield or use his speed and his bunting ability to beat out hits. He made himself into a tough out.

Compare Smith's statistics from the first seven years of his career with the next nine years and the improvement is dramatic. In his first seven years, he batted over .250 just twice and had more than 150 hits once. In the next nine years, he never batted less than .250 and was consistently in the .280 range. All from hard work and baseball savvy.

Take 1987, Ozzie's best year with the bat. He had 182 hits and a .303 batting average, 61 more hits and 55 points higher than his first year with the Cardinals, five years earlier. He also drove in 75 runs (32 more than in 1982), scored 104 runs, and was in the top eight in the National League in batting, games played, at-bats, runs, hits, doubles, walks, stolen bases, and sacrifice flies. And he made only 10 errors in 761 chances. Imagine! Mind-boggling!

He should have been the Most Valuable Player in the National League that year. He finished second in the voting to Andre Dawson of the Cubs, and that set off, once again, the debate on what is a Most Valuable Player. If the award is intended to go to the Player of the Year, then there's no argument.

Dawson had a fabulous year, a league-leading 49 homers, 137 RBIs, and a batting average of .287. But the Cubs finished last in the National League East and the Cards finished first.

I have always subscribed to the theory that Most Valuable means exactly that—*most valuable*. The Cubs could have finished last without Andre Dawson. The Cardinals would not have won the pennant without Ozzie Smith.

If Ozzie Smith was the prototype shortstop of his era, **Marty "Slats" Marion** was the same of his, in the forties. He was the sleek standard by which all shortstops were measured. His very name conjures up poise and élan. And his nickname, the "Octopus," is so descriptive. That was Marion, all arms and legs and tentacles that gracefully sucked up ground balls.

The standard by which all shortstops of the forties and fifties were measured: Marty "Slats" Marion, also known as the "Octopus" because he seemed to be all arms and legs.
Bettman/CORBIS

As a testimony to his greatness as a shortstop, in 1944, when the Cardinals won the National League pennant, Marion batted only .267 and drove in 63, yet he was voted the Most Valuable Player in the National League even though Bill "Swish" Nicholson of the Cubs led the league in home runs and RBIs (he had almost twice as many as Marion), Dixie Walker of the Dodgers led the league in batting; and Bucky Walters of the Reds, Mort Cooper of the Cardinals, Rip Sewell of the Pirates, and Bill Voiselle of the Giants all won 20 games. Clearly, this was a vote for defense. He ranks second on my Cardinals all-time shortstops list.

Marty Marion was such an icon in St. Louis, for years the Cardinals searched for his clone. Twenty years after Marion left the Cardinals, they thought they had found him. His name was Ray Busse and he was playing for the Houston Astros. The Cardinals traded for him for one reason—he resembled Marty Marion.

Busse was a nice guy, and he was built like Marion—6'4", 175 pounds. He was the image of Marty Marion everywhere but on the field.

One night in 1974, we were playing the Dodgers and Busse made four errors, tying the major league record for errors by a shortstop in one game. When it came to the ninth inning and we were taking the field, Busse refused to go back out there. He just refused.

"You've got to go out," said Red Schoendienst, our manager. But Busse wouldn't budge and Red didn't know what to do.

The next day, the *St. Louis Globe-Democrat* ran a story lamenting the Cardinals' lack of a shortstop. Bob Gibson read the story, threw the paper down and, in typical Gibson fashion, hilarious and purposefully profane, shouted, "We had a $#@%! shortstop, but you $#@%! got rid of him."

Gibby was talking about **Dal Maxvill**, number three on my list. Maxie had been our shortstop when we won consecutive pennants in 1967 and 1968. He was never much of a hitter, but that wasn't his true value to a team. He made all the plays in the field, and he was a winner. But the Cardinals got impatient and were looking for a shortstop that would provide more offense, so they traded Maxvill to Oakland, where he played for another pennant winner.

Instead of dwelling on the things Maxvill couldn't do, the Cardinals should have realized what they had—a terrific, steady shortstop in the Roy McMillan mold. I think the Cardinals eventually regretted trading him.

Despite his size—5′11″, 157 pounds—Dal Maxvill (right), the shortstop for the Cardinals, 1967 and 1968 pennant winners, was extremely tough physically. *AP/Wide World Photos*

Maxie was smart as a whip. One of the most intelligent, most honorable, most engaging people I have ever met. You couldn't meet Dal Maxvill, in a baseball uniform or in an office as the Cardinals' general manager, and not have the highest regard for him. I couldn't be more sincere in saying that.

Maxie had an engineering degree from Washington University in St. Louis. I roomed with him, and he would talk to me ad nauseam about engineering. I never had any idea what he was talking about. Many a night he put me to sleep trying to explain the difference between fuses and circuit breakers.

As a player, Maxie had grit and determination beyond compare. He's a little guy, but he was as physically tough as any player I've ever known. He didn't back down from anybody. Not anybody!

The Cardinals made him their general manager, and because of his intelligence, his charm, his ability to get along with people, and his knowledge of the game, he would have been a great one. But he was saddled with constraints that made it impossible for him to succeed. At the time the Cardinals were in an economy wave, and they told Maxvill there would be no new contracts. Maxie had promised Joe Torre that he would return as the manager, but the Cardinals, in effect, said no new contracts.

"As a player, Maxie had grit and determination beyond compare."

"But I gave him my word," Maxvill argued. "We shook hands on it."

The club still refused to honor that verbal agreement, so Maxie resigned as general manager.

When Torre became manager of the Yankees, he arranged to get Maxvill a job as a scout in the St. Louis area. He would go to Cardinals games and file reports on National League teams. Then the Yankees wanted to expand his area, but Maxvill told them if they did, he would quit. They insisted, but again Maxvill wouldn't back down. He resigned and gave back the money the Yankees had paid him.

In 1964, the Cardinals ended an 18-year drought by winning the National League pennant. They did it largely because of the contributions of an All-Star infield. Bill White was the first baseman, Julian Javier was the second baseman, Ken Boyer was the third baseman, and **Dick Groat** was the shortstop.

Groat had been an All-America basketball player at Duke University, one of the greatest players in their history. He probably could have been a star in professional basketball, but when he graduated, in the early fifties, the NBA still was in its infancy and they weren't paying the big money basketball players are getting today. So Groat, who had been an All-America baseball player as well, signed with the Pittsburgh Pirates and was a key member of their 1960 World Series championship team that beat the Yankees on Bill Mazeroski's home run in the bottom of the ninth of the seventh game.

We were teammates for only three seasons, but I learned more about base running from Dick Groat, shown here picking Mickey Mantle off second base in the 1964 World Series, than from anybody else. *Bettman/CORBIS*

Groat, my number four pick, came to the Cardinals in a trade after the 1962 season. We were teammates for only three years, but I learned more about base running from him than from anybody else.

I once asked Don Zimmer, who has been in baseball for 60 years, if he believed that more games were won and lost on the bases than any other phase of the game and he said he did. To me, Dick Groat epitomized the player who could win a game, or avoid losing a game, with his base running.

Dick wasn't fast, but he maximized his base-running ability better than anyone I've ever seen. I learned theory and practicality from him. I never saw anybody as good as Groat going from first to third. He did everything instinctively on the bases. I never saw him get thrown out going from first to third.

At bat, Dick was a great contact hitter and a great situational hitter who usually put the ball in play. He would take the first strike 85 percent of the time, and he was as good a two-strike hitter as I've ever seen.

"I never saw anybody as good as Groat going from first to third. He did everything instinctively on the bases."

Defensively, he wasn't flashy, but he was sure-handed and steady. He made all the routine plays, which is what pitchers like. They don't care so much about the spectacular play, just make the routine play. With Groat, you never left the field saying a ball that was hit to shortstop should have been caught. Dick Groat always caught the ball.

Growing up in the Cardinals organization, I learned to appreciate the importance of good fundamentals and making the routine plays, doing the little things you must do to win ballgames. I had two mentors with the Cardinals to whom I am indebted, George Kissell and Eddie Stanky. I never knew two people who not only knew so much about baseball but also had the ability to teach the game.

The Cardinals taught you how to play the game, and they taught you how to think the game, which might explain why so many ex-Cardinals become managers and broadcasters.

One ex-Cardinal who became a manager and a broadcaster was **Leo Durocher**, who put the "gas" in the Gashouse Gang. You can take that any way you want. Leo, number five on my list of all-time Cardinals shortstops, was a weak hitter, but he was a slick fielder who would try any trick to beat you. He also was a self-promoter with an annoying panache. I knew Leo. He was a great storyteller, and a great *storyteller*, if you get my meaning.

By all accounts, Durocher was a scoundrel. There are stories of him taking money out of the players' valuables box in the clubhouse. And there's that infamous story that when he played with the Yankees in the twenties, he stole Babe Ruth's watch.

Durocher was an unsavory character with a horrible reputation. He was suspended from baseball in 1947 for consorting with known gamblers. One can only imagine what might have happened if Bart Giamatti was commissioner of baseball at the time. But Pete Rose is not in the Hall of Fame and Leo Durocher is.

"Leo the Lip." It is not an endearing sobriquet.

During his playing days, Leo the "Lip" Durocher was a good-field, no-hit shortstop for the Cardinals—and a scoundrel. *AP/Wide World Photos*

Statistical Summaries

All statistics are for player's Cardinals career only.

HITTING

G = Games

H = Hits

HR = Home runs

RBI = Runs batted in

SB = Stolen bases

BA = Batting average

Shortstop	Years	G	H	HR	RBI	SB	BA
Ozzie Smith *Career high 75 RBI (0 HR) in 1987*	1982–96	1,990	1,944	27	664	433	.272
Marty Marion *Led N.L. with 38 doubles in 1942*	1940–50	1,502	1,402	34	605	35	.264
Dal Maxvill *First major leaguer to hit grand slam homer in Canada (4-14-69)*	1962–72	1,205	678	6	231	7	.220

(continued)	Years	G	H	HR	RBI	SB	BA
Dick Groat *One of three Cards with 200 hits in 1963 (also Curt Flood and Bill White)*	1963–65	472	536	7	195	6	.289
Leo Durocher *Raised his batting average each year from 1933–36*	1933–37	683	611	15	294	21	.255

FIELDING

PO = Put-outs

A = Assists

E = Errors

DP = Double plays

TC/G = Total chances divided by games played

FA = Fielding average

Shortstop	PO	A	E	DP	TC/G	FA
Ozzie Smith	3,221	6,229	196	1,221	5.0	.980
Marty Marion	2,881	4,691	247	937	5.3	.968
Dal Maxvill	1,595	3,050	129	575	4.5	.973
Dick Groat	748	1,397	93	268	4.8	.958
Leo Durocher	1,450	1,958	134	383	5.2	.962

FIVE

Third Baseman

Who's the best third baseman in Cardinals history? To me, that's a no-brainer. My choice is **Kenton Lloyd "Ken" Boyer**, although I have to wonder how long it will take Albert Pujols to rise to the top of the list. In 2001, his rookie season, Pujols batted .329, hit 37 home runs, drove in 130 runs—better numbers than Boyer had in any one season—and was named National League Rookie of the Year. If he keeps that up, he could become the Cardinals' all-time third baseman. But one season is not enough to rate him among the top five Cardinals third basemen of all-time just yet, particularly since Tony LaRussa spread Pujols' talents around in left and right field and first base.

Boyer was the captain of the championship Cardinals team in 1964, and he would remain the "Captain" to his teammates forever, just as Pee Wee Reese, the solid shortstop of the great Dodgers teams of the fifties, was always the "Captain" to his teammates.

Boyer came from a baseball family and was the middle of three brothers who played in the major leagues. His older brother, Cloyd, pitched for the

1. KENTON LLOYD "KEN" BOYER

2. GEORGE "WHITEY" KUROWSKI

3. TERRY PENDLETON

4. JOE TORRE

5. JOHNNY LEONARD ROOSEVELT "PEPPER" MARTIN

Cardinals and the Kansas City Athletics and later was a pitching coach for the Yankees. His younger brother, Clete, played for the Yankees in the sixties and was considered one of the greatest fielding third basemen ever, on par with his contemporary, Hall of Famer Brooks Robinson.

Brother opposed brother when the Yankees and the Cardinals met in the 1964 World Series. With the Yanks up 3–0 in Game 4, Kenny hit a grand slam and we won, 4–3. Kenny and Clete both homered in Game 7, but the Cardinals won, 7–5, and took the Series. It is the only time in baseball history brothers hit home runs in the same World Series game.

The "Captain," the late Ken Boyer—my teammate, my friend, and my choice as the number one third baseman in Cardinals history. *Bettman/CORBIS*

*C*hester Vern and Mabel Agnes Boyer of Alba, Missouri, produced 14 children—seven girls and seven boys—three of whom played major league baseball. Cloyd Victor Boyer, the third child, first boy, pitched for five seasons with the St. Louis Cardinals and the Kansas City Athletics; Kenton Lloyd Boyer, the fifth child, third boy, had a 15-year career with the Cardinals, the New York Mets, the Chicago White Sox, and the Los Angeles Dodgers; and Cletis Leroy Boyer, the eighth child, fifth boy, played for 16 years with the Athletics, the New York Yankees, and the Atlanta Braves.

"Ken was my idol," said Clete Boyer, six years his brother's junior. "I didn't get to see him play a lot except for a few games on television, or on the opposing team in spring-training games and one World Series, but I know what kind of player he was. He could run, he could throw, he could hit, and he could think. He was a quiet leader. People say I was a better third baseman than he was, but I can't believe I was. Maybe I had better hands, but Ken could do everything else at third. And he could hit. In a 10-year period, he had 40 more RBIs than Mickey Mantle.

"If we changed places and Ken played in New York, he'd be in the Hall of Fame today. It's like Roberto Clemente. He was by far the greatest defensive right fielder who ever lived, but because he played in Pittsburgh, he didn't get the credit he deserved. I played with Roger Maris and against Al Kaline, and they were both great right fielders. But they weren't in Clemente's class."

The Boyers raised their brood in a 1,000-square-foot home. "We had no electricity until I reached the fourth grade," said Clete, "but we had a ballpark, and baseball was our life."

Young Ken Boyer played in the Ban Johnson League. Clete was the team's batboy. Mickey Mantle was in the same league.

"Mickey was from Oklahoma and we were from Missouri, but we were only 25 miles apart," said Clete. "Mickey and Ken were the two big athletes in our area at the time. They were the same age [actually Ken was exactly five months to the day older than Mick]. Mickey got a $1,500 bonus when he signed with the Yankees. Ken got $8,000 when he signed with the Cardinals."

In 1964 the Yankees won the American League pennant, the Cardinals won in the National League, and they met in the World Series. It was the first time brothers played on opposing teams in a World Series, both at third base.

"How great that was," said Clete. "My parents came to the games. I know they were rooting for Ken because I was playing in my fifth World Series and that was Ken's first. But Joe Garagiola interviewed my dad and asked him who he was rooting for and he said, 'I'm just pulling for the third baseman.'

"Ken and I would get together for dinner after the games. We'd talk about baseball in general, but never about the World Series specifically.

"When he dropped a pop fly in Yankee Stadium, I left him a note that said, 'You have to watch the air pockets here.' Then in St. Louis, he hit a smash past me, and Ken left me a note that said, 'You have to watch the hops on this infield.'

"That World Series was the most fun I ever had playing baseball. It was like I'm trying to show my big brother, my idol, how good I am, and he's trying to show me how good he is. To me, that is the way baseball is supposed to be.

"Then when he hit the grand slam in Game 4, that was the greatest thing. We were leading 3–0 at the time, and if we won that game, it would have put us up three games to one in the World Series. But Ken hits the home run and they win the game, and even though it tied the Series, I couldn't help feeling so much pride for my brother. When he hit that home run, it was like 'This Is Your Life, the Boyer Family.'

"They used to say about Mickey Mantle that he was a celebrity in his own clubhouse. That's the same with Ken. He was a celebrity in his own clubhouse, and a hero in his own family."

Game 4 was played in Yankee Stadium. Ken's grand slam came in the sixth inning with the Yankees leading 3–0. Al Downing threw him a changeup, and Kenny drilled it into the lower seats in left field. When the ball left the park, the stadium grew quiet, but there was plenty of excitement in our dugout. We were yelling and cheering, and we all rose and moved to the home-plate side of the third-base dugout to greet Ken as he circled the bases.

I happened to be watching Kenny as he rounded second. It seemed to me that he slowed down noticeably as he was about to reach third. Then, as he passed third, I saw Clete reach out and unobtrusively give Ken a pat on the backside with his glove. I thought that was a very touching gesture for Clete to make, and it showed the affection the brothers had for one another.

Though perhaps not quite the fielder Clete was, Ken was outstanding in every facet of the game, a lifetime .287 hitter with almost 300 home runs and more than 1,100 RBIs. Those are close to Hall of Fame numbers, but Ken never made it to Cooperstown even though his instincts, intelligence, and base-running abilities were crème de la crème.

Boyer was signed originally as a pitcher, but his pitching in the minor leagues showed little promise. However, his bat impressed the Cardinals enough for them to convert him to third base, just as a couple of decades earlier the Cardinals converted another pitcher to the outfield. His name was Stan Musial.

After his first two seasons with the Cardinals, Boyer was tried in center field. When Curt Flood came along, Kenny went back to third, and that turned out to be good for both Boyer and the Cardinals. With great range to his left and a powerful and accurate arm, Boyer won five Gold Gloves at third base. Unfortunately for Ken, he was traded to the Mets after the 1965 season, so he missed the Cardinals' championship seasons of 1967 and 1968.

I consider myself fortunate to have played with the two premier National League third basemen of their eras, Ken Boyer in St. Louis and Mike Schmidt in Philadelphia.

Sadly, Ken Boyer left us all too soon. He died in 1982 of lung cancer. He was only 51. I still miss him, and I will always remember the "Captain" fondly.

Clete has said that Ken was the hero of his family. Kenny was also the hero of my family: my baseball family.

George "Whitey" Kurowski is second on my list. He was one of the Cardinals heroes and one of the great baseball names of my youth. He played nine seasons in the major leagues, all with the Cardinals, all in the forties. His two-run home run off Hall of Famer Red Ruffing in the top of the ninth of Game 5 of the 1942 World Series gave the Cardinals a 4–2 victory over the Yankees and the World Series championship, four games to one.

As a boy, Kurowski had osteomyelitis, which resulted in his right arm being shorter than his left; but he still became one of the best third basemen of the forties. He had his best year in 1947, when he hit 27 home runs and

When I was growing up as a Cardinals fan in Memphis, George "Whitey" Kurowski, my number two all-time Cards third baseman, was one of the magic names of my youth.
AP/Wide World Photos

knocked in 104 runs. The following year, at the peak of his career, he suffered an arm injury. The year after that he injured his elbow. Those injuries shortened his career and prevented him from compiling even greater numbers.

Third on my list is **Terry Pendleton**, the switch-hitting third baseman of the 1985 and 1987 National League championship teams. Terry actually came through the Cardinals' minor league system as a second baseman, but when he got to St. Louis, they needed a third baseman and they put Pendleton there. Good move.

Terry Pendleton didn't have great speed, but he stole 24 bases for the Cardinals in 1986.
Lew Portnoy, Spectra-Action, Inc.

Terry became one of the best fielding third basemen in the game. He had quick hands, the necessary quick first two steps, and a more-than-adequate arm. At bat, he was a solid contact hitter and a good base runner. Despite a lack of blazing speed, he stole 24 bases in 1986. Pendleton actually had his best years when he left the Cardinals and played for the Braves, but his seven seasons in St. Louis were productive enough for him to make my all-time Cardinals team.

I can't say I'm surprised that **Joe Torre** became a successful major league manager, but I'd be less than honest if I said I thought he would have so much success as manager of the New York Yankees. He's a good bet to be elected to the Hall of Fame.

Torre came to the Cardinals in 1969 in a trade with the Atlanta Braves for Orlando Cepeda, straight up, and we were teammates and roommates for two years, until I was traded to the Red Sox. I came to know Joe as a man of intelligence, grace, and compassion. His knowledge of baseball and his unique people skills made him a good bet to succeed as a manager. We even whimsically discussed being comanagers one day.

When we got Torre, he had already enjoyed a successful nine-year career with the Braves in Milwaukee and Atlanta and had developed into one of the best pure hitters in the game. He was just 29 when the Cardinals got him, and his best years as a hitter were ahead of him.

Joe started his career as a catcher, and he was a good one. After a few years, the Braves recognized Torre's value as a hitter and realized the wear and tear of catching would erode his batting skills, so they weaned him off catching and played him part-time at first base.

When the Cardinals traded for him, their idea was that Joe would be Cepeda's replacement at first base, but they also had him for emergency duty behind the plate. I believe that Joe's experience as a catcher, and the five years he worked as a broadcaster for the Anaheim (then California) Angels, helped him hone his managerial skills.

In Torre's second year in St. Louis, the Cardinals had a promising young left-handed power hitter named Joe Hague who they wanted to try at first base. And Mike Shannon, who had shifted successfully from the outfield to third base and was the third baseman on our championship teams in 1967 and 1968, was suffering from nephritis, an acute inflammation of the kidneys.

The malady was so serious, his career was doomed. Consequently, Torre split his time between catching and third base, a position he had never played in the major leagues. He was so determined, fearless, and hardworking, and he took to the position so well, the Cardinals converted him to third base full time in 1971. It turned out to be Torre's best year.

Dal Maxvill said of Joe, "He's not just a guy who made the switch to third base, he became a damn good third baseman."

Before he became the successful manager of the Yankees (and lost those muttonchops), Joe Torre was a dangerous hitter who won a batting title and was named National League Most Valuable Player with the Cardinals in 1971. *AP/Wide World Photos*

In 1971, I was no longer Torre's teammate, so I didn't get to see him every day. I was with the Phillies that year, so I did get to see him as an opponent. I haven't seen many hitters have the kind of year Torre had. It seemed he hit the ball hard three or four times a game. He had a league-leading 230 hits, and if you saw Joe play, you know because of his lack of speed, he had few leg hits. He led the league in batting with a .363 average and in RBIs with 137, and he was voted the National League's Most Valuable Player.

The next year, the Cardinals started grooming a new third baseman, an outstanding fielder named Ken Reitz. Hague had failed to live up to his promise, so the Cards moved Torre back to first base, and he split his time between first and third. By 1972 he was a first baseman almost full time, with a few games sprinkled in at third and catcher.

Altogether, Torre played slightly more than 400 games at third base for the Cardinals, but in his six years in St. Louis, he was so productive, he deserves a place on their all-time team at some position. He could be listed among the catchers or the first basemen. I choose to list him fourth among Cardinals third basemen because it was at that position that he had his best year.

After the 1974 season, Torre was traded to the Mets. Three years later, they made him their manager. He lacked managerial experience, and he inherited a terrible team, so his record as manager of the Mets is poor. In four-and-a-half seasons, he didn't have one winning season.

The Mets fired him after 1981, and the Braves hired him immediately to be their manager. Amazingly, he won a division title in his first year with the Braves, 1982. Maybe not so amazingly: better players plus better team equals success. Also, Joe had those four-and-a-half years of experience with the Mets as a training ground to managing.

Unfortunately, in Atlanta, Joe never had the support of the Braves' maverick owner, Ted Turner. After three seasons (one first-place finish, two seconds), Joe thought he deserved a contract extension. Turner thought he deserved to be fired.

After Atlanta, Torre spent five years as a broadcaster/analyst for the Angels, which proved to be a fortunate happenstance in contributing to his future success as a manager. In the broadcast booth, he could step back, study, and analyze the game from afar to gain a better understanding of what it takes to be a successful manager, without the pressure of wins and losses. He was on the other side of the mirror, questioning, not being questioned. This would prove invaluable when he took the Yankees job in 1996.

However, before going to the Yankees Joe got another chance to manage when the Cardinals hired him at the end of the 1990 season. He managed in St. Louis for five seasons and had the Cardinals in contention every year, but he never won, largely because the club was operated on a shoestring and they refused to spend the money necessary to win.

When the Cardinals fired him during the 1995 season, Torre thought his managing days were over. He sought to get back into broadcasting. He was surprised, and so was everybody else, when he was hired by George Steinbrenner to manage the Yankees. He wasn't even Steinbrenner's first choice, and the media took a cynical view of the selection of Torre, referring to him as "Clueless Joe." Few, except those who knew him, expected him to last in the job for more than a year, much less achieve such remarkable success.

"Timing is everything. Torre had become the culmination of his playing, managing, and broadcasting experiences. After years of doubt and unsureness, Joe exploded into a prominence few managers have enjoyed."

It's one of the great baseball ironies that the so-called Clueless Joe, who was 109 games under .500 in three managerial stints with the Mets, Braves, and Cardinals, should find such success working in the grand stage that is New York for an owner as demanding as George Steinbrenner.

Timing is everything. Torre had become the culmination of his playing, managing, and broadcasting experiences. After years of doubt and unsureness, Joe exploded into a prominence few managers have enjoyed. In his first six seasons with the Yankees he won 582 games, including a staggering 114 in 1998, a Yankee record. In those six years he won five division titles, five pennants, and four World Series. He had the perfect demeanor to deal with Steinbrenner, his star players, and the press. He reveled in his newfound celebrity with grace and class.

When we were teammates he used to tell me that he wished he could release his anger as easily as some. Too many things built up inside. Now, if you look at Joe in the dugout, sitting calmly, chewing on a peach pit, never changing his expression, it might seem that he's calm and cool. But what you see outside is rarely what is going on inside.

One of the most colorful, flamboyant and daring players—and one of the best names—in baseball history was **Johnny Leonard Roosevelt "Pepper" Martin**, known as the "Wild Horse of the Osage" for his aggressive style of play. Perhaps more than any other Cardinal, he personified the Gashouse

71

Pepper Martin, the "Wild Horse of the Osage," personified the hell-for-leather, aggressive play of the Cardinals' famed "Gashouse Gang" of the thirties. He was a star at two positions: third base and center field. *AP/Wide World Photos*

Gang. He slid on his belly before it was fashionable, he ran hard all the time, and he played every game with abandon.

Martin never played in the minor leagues. He came directly to the Cardinals and made an immediate impression with his passionate play. He's another who, like Joe Torre, could be listed among the all-time Cardinals at more than one position. He was their regular center fielder when they won the 1931 World Series. In fact, he was the star of that World Series with a .500 average and five stolen bases against the Philadelphia Athletics. He was also their regular third baseman in the 1934 World Series.

Martin had two hits in Game 7, scored three runs, and stole two bases against the Tigers' manager and Hall of Fame catcher, the great Mickey Cochrane. The Cards went on to win the game—and the Series—with a final score of 11–0.

That winter, Martin's seventh game performance was immortalized at the annual New York Baseball Writers dinner. It was before my time, of course, but I have heard that it was the custom of the New York writers to stage a show at their annual dinner with parodies of popular songs that depicted events of the baseball season.

A writer, posing as Martin, sang the following parody, to the tune of "Goodnight Sweetheart."

"Good-bye Mickey, this is Pepper Martin,
I'm on first base, soon I will be startin'.
Off to second I'll fly like a bird.
Then in a word, I think I'll steal third.
So I say good-bye Mickey,
Put your mitt and mask on,
If your jockstrap's loose, better put another clasp on.
The way I feel, there's nothing I won't steal.
So good-bye Mickey, good-bye."

Statistical Summaries

All statistics are for player's Cardinals career only.

HITTING

G = Games

H = Hits

HR = Home runs

RBI = Runs batted in

SB = Stolen bases

BA = Batting average

Third Baseman	Years	G	H	HR	RBI	SB	BA
Ken Boyer *Twice hit for the cycle (9-14-61, 6-16-64)*	1955–65	1,667	1,855	255	1,001	97	.293
Whitey Kurowski *Led N.L. in putouts three times and twice in fielding percentage*	1941–49	916	925	106	529	19	.286
Terry Pendleton *Hit .429 as a designated hitter in 1987 World Series vs. Minnesota*	1984–90	768	888	44	442	99	.259

(continued)	Years	G	H	HR	RBI	SB	BA
Joe Torre *Drove in 100 runs each of his first three seasons with Cards*	1969–74	918	1,062	98	558	12	.308
Pepper Martin *Career World Series average of .418 is highest of any player*	1928 1930–40 1944	1,189	1,227	59	501	146	.298

FIELDING

PO = Put-outs

A = Assists

E = Errors

DP = Double plays

TC/G = Total chances divided by games played

FA = Fielding average

Third Baseman	PO	A	E	DP	TC/G	FA
Ken Boyer	1,373	3,149	225	306	3.1	.953
Whitey Kurowski	1,025	1,569	116	137	3.1	.957
Terry Pendleton	717	2,135	123	155	3.2	.959
Joe Torre	362	673	53	55	2.5	.951
Pepper Martin	393	715	87	44	2.8	.927

SIX

Left Fielder

A<small>RRIVE AT</small> B<small>USCH</small> S<small>TADIUM</small> in St. Louis and, chances are, the first thing you will see is a huge bronze statue of **Stan Musial** in his famous, unorthodox, peek-a-boo batting style—crouched low, peering at the pitcher as if he were looking around a corner, the bat held high and perpendicular to the ground.

It's only fitting that one should be greeted by Stan the Man, because few baseball players in history are as synonymous with one city and one team as Musial is with St. Louis and the Cardinals, for whom he played his entire career, 22 seasons, not including one year in military service. He also served one year as the Cards' general manager, was a senior vice president of the Cardinals for more than a quarter of a century, has been a St. Louis resident for more than six decades, and was co-owner of a popular St. Louis landmark, Stan & Biggie's Restaurant.

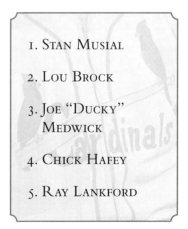

1. S<small>TAN</small> M<small>USIAL</small>

2. L<small>OU</small> B<small>ROCK</small>

3. J<small>OE</small> "D<small>UCKY</small>" M<small>EDWICK</small>

4. C<small>HICK</small> H<small>AFEY</small>

5. R<small>AY</small> L<small>ANKFORD</small>

Unlike most other great stars of the game, Stan's entire baseball association has been with the St. Louis Cardinals. Babe Ruth, for example, played for two Boston teams and coached in Brooklyn. Ty Cobb played in Detroit and Philadelphia. Joe DiMaggio coached in Oakland. Hank Aaron played in Atlanta and Milwaukee, Willie Mays in San Francisco and New York. Ted Williams managed in Washington. Even Bob Gibson coached in Atlanta and New York.

But Stan Musial was and is first, last, and always a St. Louis Cardinal. This Cardinal would, and should, be the Pope (he's Polish like Pope John Paul, who happens to be a good friend of Stan's). He is one of the most universally loved sports figures ever, except in Brooklyn, where he was viewed with grudging respect because of the way he terrorized the Dodgers, repeatedly peppering the short right-field wall in Brooklyn's Ebbets Field. It was the Dodgers fans that tagged him with his famous nickname, "Stan the Man."

The first time I saw Musial was in 1960, my first spring training with the Cardinals. I was 18 years old and I was in awe of him. I'll never forget seeing him arrive in spring training with a trunk for his clothes. No luggage, just a trunk. I couldn't believe a player would bring a trunk to spring training.

His first day in camp, I was catching batting practice and Stan stepped into the cage to take his first swings of the spring. He watched as three pitches went by, just missing the front corner of the plate. And with each pitch, Stan would say, "No, that's outside . . . No, that's not a strike . . ."

I was amazed. It's easier to judge the strike zone high and low than it is inside and outside, but here he was 39 years old, he hadn't stepped in a batter's box in five months, yet his eyes were tuned to midseason form.

Right from the start, I seemed to hit it off with Stan. He was paternalistic toward me, I think, because his son, Dick, had attended Christian Brothers College High School in St. Louis, and I went to Christian Brothers High School in Memphis, so it was kind of a shepherding feeling.

Stan's career is well documented. He came out of a small Pennsylvania steel-mill town and signed with the Cardinals as a pitcher. At Daytona Beach, his manager was Dickie Kerr, who had pitched for the Chicago White Sox in the 1919 World Series. That was the year of the so-called Black Sox scandal, when eight members of the White Sox were accused of conspiring to throw the World Series to the Cincinnati Reds and, although they were never convicted, the eight men were banned from baseball for life. Kerr was not one of the purported cheaters. In fact, he pitched two complete-game victories for the White Sox in that World Series.

Under Kerr, Musial won 18 games, was also used as an outfielder, and batted over .350. One day, Musial made a diving catch in the outfield and landed

Stan the "Man" Musial is the greatest Cardinal of them all. And in St. Louis he's more than that—he's like the Pope.
AP/Wide World Photos

heavily on his left shoulder. That was the end of a promising pitching career but the beginning of one of the great hitting careers in baseball history. Like Babe Ruth, Musial switched from pitching to the outfield and batted his way into the Hall of Fame.

He won seven batting titles, had a lifetime average of .331, and drove in more than 100 runs 10 times. Later in his career, Stan became a home-run threat, often hitting more than 30 a season. In 1948, he missed the triple crown by one home run.

One of the things about Musial's career that stands out is his remarkable consistency. He batted .310 or higher for 16 consecutive seasons, had two fewer runs scored in his career than he drove in, and in one of the great statistical quirks, had exactly the same number of hits at home as he did on the road.

I can't say Musial was the greatest hitter I ever saw. After all, I caught him at the end of his career. But I will say this. He probably was the greatest low-ball hitter ever. Even in his forties, there was no more devastating a low-ball hitter than Stan. Throw him a pitch down in the strike zone, even below the zone, and he would leave his feet.

As great as Musial was, as celebrated as he was, he would have reached legendary proportions if he had played in New York. Imagine him in Yankee Stadium, with the right-field fence being as short as it was; he would have hit many more home runs and he would have been at least as big as DiMaggio.

Musial's last year was 1963, my first full season. The Cardinals traded Gene Oliver on June 15 and made me their number one catcher. I was doing very well, and one day Musial said he wanted to talk to me. Wow, I thought, the great man has noticed me. He probably wants to give me a pat on the back or pass along some batting tip. I thought that was very special.

"Tim," Musial said, "I'd like you to speed up your at-bats."

I was awestruck. In all the years I've known him that was the only thing Stan ever said or did that disappointed me. It was an aberration. Except for that one glitch, Stan is everything his legend and his persona say he is and then some. He's an extraordinary man in a lot of ways; he's one of the genuinely nicest people I know.

Second to Stan Musial as a Cardinals left fielder is the man who replaced the great Stan the Man, **Lou Brock**, who came to the Cards from the Cubs in one of baseball's greatest trades from a Cardinals perspective, but one the Cubs didn't live down for years.

It wasn't perceived as such an important trade at the time, June 15, 1964. It was a six-man trade, but it essentially came down to Brock for Ernie Broglio, who had won 21 games in 1960 and 18 in 1963. Meanwhile, Brock had had two mediocre seasons in Chicago, although he did show flashes of power for a man his size, 5'11", 170 pounds. He is one of only three players to hit a ball into the center-field seats in the old Polo Grounds in New York, more than 450 feet from home plate. The others were Hank Aaron and Joe Adcock.

There was enormous pressure on Lou when he joined us midway through the 1964 season. Not only was he playing the position previously held down by the great Stan Musial, to get him we had traded away a proven winner in Broglio, who had won 60 games in the previous four seasons.

Johnny Keane, the Cardinals' manager, helped Brock make the transition by instilling confidence in him immediately. He put him in left field and batted him in the leadoff spot, and Brock paid big dividends. When we got him, Lou was hitting .251 for the Cubs. He batted .348 for us, and since we won the pennant by one game over the Phillies and the Reds and three over the Giants in the closest race in National League history, it's safe to say we would not have won had we not acquired Brock.

We clinched the pennant on the final day of the season and celebrated raucously in our clubhouse. One reporter spotted Stan Musial, who had retired the year before. The reporter went up to him and said, "Too bad you didn't play one more year, Stan. You could have been part of this."

In what may be the greatest trade in Cardinals history, Lou Brock came from the Cubs, then helped us win three National League pennants, broke the all-time stolen-base record, and was elected to the Hall of Fame. *AP/Wide World Photos*

Always the epitome of class, Musial said, "If I had played one more year, we wouldn't have won the pennant, because then we wouldn't have traded for Lou Brock."

As a postscript, Broglio won only four games for the Cubbies in 1964.

Brock went on to have a brilliant Hall of Fame career with the Cardinals. He gave us a whole new dimension with his speed and base-stealing ability. He made a thorough study of the art of stealing bases.

Brock had the most explosive start at first base of any player I've ever seen. I don't ever remember him diving back to first. He took long leads off first but always was able to get back in time without diving, which saved a lot of wear and tear on his body.

With the Cardinals, Lou won eight stolen-base championships, broke Maury Wills' National League record of 104 stolen bases when he swiped 118 in 1974, was the first man to steal 100 bases at the age of 35, and was the major league's all-time stolen-base leader (a record that has since been surpassed by Rickey Henderson).

"Medwick was the left fielder of the Gashouse Gang, with all the characteristics that their name and reputation implies: a ruthless, vicious, hard-nosed player, and a good one."

Discussing **Joe "Ducky" Medwick** after talking about Musial's grace and gentility may be unfortunate. While Musial is a beloved figure in baseball, Medwick was crude and surly.

I heard a story that when Bing Devine, who would have two tours of duty as the Cardinals' general manager, was a young man, starting out his career in the Cardinals' front office, Medwick treated him like dirt. Devine never forgot that, and years later, when Medwick was looking for a job with the Cardinals, Bing refused to hire him.

Nevertheless, Medwick deserves to be listed among the best left fielders in Cardinals' history. I place him third on my list.

Medwick was the left fielder of the Gashouse Gang, with all the characteristics that their name and reputation implies: a ruthless, vicious, hard-nosed player, and a good one. He was a notorious bad-ball hitter with a lifetime batting average of .324 and was the last National Leaguer to win the triple crown, in 1937.

82

Joe "Ducky" Medwick was ruthless and vicious on the field, crude and surly off the field, and a mainstay of the "Gashouse Gang." He was elected to the Hall of Fame in 1968.
AP/Wide World Photos

He was before my time, but I didn't have to see
Chick Hafey to be impressed with his lifetime .317
average, three plus-100 RBI seasons, and three
seasons of more than 20 home runs—when that
was considered a lot. Imagine how great he could
have been if he didn't have a chronic sinus
condition, poor eyesight as a result of
several beanings that made him one
of the first men to play baseball
wearing glasses, and constant
contract disputes. He still
made the Hall of Fame.

Bettman/CORBIS

Perhaps it's unfair, but typical, that despite a brilliant playing career that earned him election to the Hall of Fame, Medwick is best remembered for an incident in the seventh game of the 1934 World Series between the Cardinals and the Detroit Tigers.

With the Cards leading 7–0 in the top of the sixth, Medwick drove one off the right-field fence and raced around the bases. Even though there was no throw, Medwick slid hard into third base and upended Tigers third base-man Marv Owen. The two scuffled on the ground and the partisan Detroit crowd booed Medwick unmercifully. When he went to left field in the bot-tom of the sixth, Tigers fans pelted him with bottles, food, and garbage. Finally, after five minutes, Commissioner Kenesaw Mountain Landis ordered Medwick removed from the game for his own protection. After a 20-minute delay, the game resumed and the Cardinals, with Dizzy Dean, completed an 11–0 shutout to win the game and the Series.

I don't know much about my number four man, **Chick Hafey**, except that he's another of the many players whose name is inextricably linked with Cardinals lore. He had a lifetime batting average of .317 and was elected to the Hall of Fame despite chronic ill health, poor eyesight, and frequent salary disputes, which eventually got him traded from the Cardinals to the Reds. Isn't it amazing how often salary disputes enter into the merits of judging a player, even way back in 1931?

Like Babe Ruth and Stan Musial, Hafey started as a pitcher and was converted to the outfield because of his bat, and he was one of the hardest-hitting right-handed hitters in the game. A serious sinus condition required several operations, and after he was beaned in 1926, Hafey suffered from blurred vision and was advised by a doctor to wear glasses when he played. He became one of the first bespectacled players in baseball history.

After 11 years with the Cardinals, **Ray Lankford** was shipped to San Diego in 2001 in uncharacteristically graceless fashion. While he was a Cardinal, he made their top 10 list in six offensive categories, including home runs, RBIs, and stolen bases.

Ray could hit for power and he could hit for average, and he was a consistent base-stealing threat. He was a lethal low-ball hitter on whom you

Ray Lankford was a lethal low-ball hitter who produced good numbers in a career that started in St. Louis. *AP/Wide World Photos*

had to go up the ladder, meaning each pitch had to be higher than the last. He would hammer the low pitch, but you could get him out with high, hard stuff.

Ray, fifth on my list, was a productive player for the Cardinals. Graceful exits for long time players should be the norm. Unfortunately, often they are not.

Statistical Summaries

All statistics are for player's Cardinals career only.

HITTING

G = Games

H = Hits

HR = Home runs

RBI = Runs batted in

SB = Stolen bases

BA = Batting average

Left Fielder	Years	G	H	HR	RBI	SB	BA
Stan Musial *Missed only 17 games (of 1,689) from 1946–56*	1941–44 1946–63	3,026	3,630	475	1,951	78	.331
Lou Brock *First N.L. player to have 20 homers and 50 steals in same season (1967)*	1964–79	2,289	2,713	129	814	888	.297
Joe Medwick *Averaged 228 hits a year from 1935–37*	1932–40 1947–48	1,216	1,590	152	923	28	.335

(continued)	Years	G	H	HR	RBI	SB	BA
Chick Hafey *Had hits in 10 consecutive at-bats in 1929*	1924–31	812	963	127	618	56	.326
Ray Lankford *Led majors with 15 triples in 1991*	1990–2001 1930–40	1,488	1,428	222	807	248	.274

FIELDING

PO = Put-outs

A = Assists

E = Errors

DP = Double plays

TC/G = Total chances divided by games played

FA = Fielding average

Left Fielder	PO	A	E	DP	TC/G	FA
Stan Musial	3,730	130	64	27	2.1	.984
Lou Brock	3,790	110	173	19	1.8	.958
Joe Medwick	2,531	88	64	18	2.3	.976
Chick Hafey	1,493	73	50	17	2.1	.969
Ray Lankford	3,313	66	53	10	2.4	.985

SEVEN

Center Fielder

M Y CHOICE FOR THE BEST center fielder in Cardinals history is a man I've never seen play, but I have heard so much about **Terry Moore** from people whose opinion I greatly respect that he gets my vote. Moore added class to an aging Gashouse Gang and was a mainstay of the great Cardinals teams of the forties. Playing between Stan Musial and Enos Slaughter, he gave the Cardinals one of the best outfields ever.

Moore was a solid hitter, but his career numbers were curtailed by three years in military service in World War II and a knee injury. As a defensive center fielder, he was considered the best in the game in his time. They didn't begin awarding the Gold Glove for defensive excellence until after Moore was out of baseball. If they had awarded the Gold Glove in his time, Terry Moore no doubt would have won it just about every year.

1. TERRY MOORE

2. CURT FLOOD

3. WILLIE MCGEE

4. JIM EDMONDS

5. PEPPER MARTIN

There should be a monument to **Curt Flood** somewhere, or a plaque in the Hall of Fame, to commemorate his enormous contribution to baseball. But it will never happen. Only a few years after his death (Curt died in 1997), he is barely remembered. If you go into any clubhouse in the major leagues and

If they had been awarding the Gold Glove for defense in the forties, Terry Moore would have won it every year. He was the best center fielder of his day and comparable to Willie Mays, according to Stan Musial. That's good enough for me. *Bettman/CORBIS*

mention Flood's name to today's players, very few of them will know who he was.

I find that appalling. They should genuflect at his name, for it was Flood who took the first steps in making it possible for players to earn the millions of dollars they're paid these days.

Free agency and arbitration, which are the reasons salaries have escalated to such lofty levels, would have happened sooner or later, with or without Flood. But Curt made it happen sooner because he was a man of courage and great principle who took a stand when it needed to be taken. And he took that stand at great personal sacrifice.

As I mentioned earlier, I had a cameo role in this momentous event, one of the most important, if not *the* most important in baseball history, because the trade that touched off the whole scenario was the one on October 7, 1969, in which the Cardinals sent Flood, Joe Hoerner, Byron Browne, and me to the Phillies for Dick Allen, Cookie Rojas, and Jerry Johnson. While the rest of us accepted the trade as part of the game, Flood refused to report, and that was the first shot fired in the war between players and owners. Sure, there were skirmishes prior to that, but nothing like the battles to come.

At the time, I didn't fully understand all the ramifications of the trade. I didn't think that it would be ultimately as large or as important as it has become. I was concerned primarily with my career and what I was going to do and how to prove myself. It was the first trade for me, and it was very emotional, as all first trades are.

For Flood, it became a cause.

Curt discussed with Marvin Miller, at the time executive director of the Major League Players Association, the possibility of filing an antitrust suit against Major League Baseball. After weeks of discussions between Flood and Miller, it was decided Flood would fly to San Juan, Puerto Rico, where the executive board of the Players Association was holding its annual meeting, to present his case to the board, made up of Jim Bunning, Gary Peters, Steve Hamilton, and Tom Haller. Here, again, I was an inadvertent witness to history.

Cookie Rojas and Jerry Johnson had been the Phillies' player representatives, but they were both sent to St. Louis in the Flood trade. I had been the Cardinals' player rep and the alternate National League representative. Since the Phillies didn't have a player rep, and I was now a Phillie, it made sense to me that I should go to Puerto Rico to represent the Phillies at the meeting.

erry Bluford Moore of Vernon, Alabama, had a meteoric, although star-crossed, career with the Cardinals. He arrived in St. Louis at the age of 23 in 1935, the year after the Cards beat the Tigers in the World Series, and took over as their regular center fielder. Before long, he had established himself as the premier defensive center fielder in the National League, the standard by which all other center fielders were measured.

He was an All-Star from 1939 through 1942, a stretch during which Moore batted .295, including a 20-game hitting streak in 1942. He captained two world championship teams, in 1942 and 1946.

In the fall of 1942, Moore entered military service, which cost him three of his most productive years. When he returned, he was no longer the hitter he had been before World War II, but his defensive skills had not eroded. The Gold Glove for defensive excellence was not awarded in Moore's day; had it been, he would have earned a den full.

Bad knees shortened Moore's career and reduced him to just 91 games in 1948. His batting average plummeted into the .230s. After the season, Moore retired. He died in 1995, but his defensive legacy lives on.

Three members of those championship Cardinals teams of 1942 and 1946 shared fond memories of Moore. Stan Musial and Enos Slaughter flanked Moore in the Cardinals' outfield. Marty Marion played in front of him at shortstop. Each of them attested to Moore's defensive brilliance.

"Terry was our team leader and captain," Musial remembered, "and a great center fielder. We all looked up to him. We often went to him with our problems, on or off the field. You can compare him with the great center fielders of all time and you'd be accurate."

Past his 86th birthday, and just weeks from his death, Hall of Famer Enos Slaughter was as spry as ever, both physically and mentally. He had almost total recall of events of his playing days and of the memories he kept of Cardinals teammates. When he spoke of Terry Moore, it was in terms of reverence and awe.

"You talk about the great center fielders of all time and Terry rates right up there with any of them," Slaughter raved. "DiMaggio, Mays, any of them.

I played against Joe DiMaggio and I played against Willie Mays, and Terry was as good as them.

"He had speed and a great arm, and nobody charged ground balls from the outfield like Moore. He'd charge the ball and make a perfect throw to third base or home. Many times I saw him slide on his belly to make a catch. The best thing about Terry is he never made a play look hard. That's what they say about DiMaggio, that he was always there waiting for a fly ball. It was the same with Terry Moore."

Marty Marion: "Terry was one of the great defensive outfielders of my time and a true leader. He was the oldest man on the team, respected by everybody. He wore a very small glove and he had great big hands. I never saw a man with bigger hands than Terry. He often would catch a ball bare-handed. I saw him do it several times.

"I'm taking nothing away from Joe DiMaggio. He was a great center fielder, but he was no better than Terry. And Joe played in New York. Willie Mays had more flair, but believe me, in center field, Terry was everything Willie was."

I flew down from Memphis and Curt from St. Louis, and we both had to stop in Atlanta to change planes. It was at the Atlanta airport that I accidentally ran into Curt. I was surprised to learn that he was going to the meeting.

It was while we were waiting in the airport that Curt filled me in on his reason for attending the meeting. He was planning to file an antitrust suit against baseball and he was hoping to get the blessing and support of the Players Association. I asked Curt at length about his plans. That's when I found out how serious he was about this whole thing, and it started to sink in that he was making a very big move indeed and that he was totally committed to it.

At the meeting, Flood laid out his plan for the executive board. All he wanted from the Players Association was that it pay the fee for a top-notch antitrust lawyer and that it cover any out-of-pocket expenses he would incur flying in from St. Louis, probably to New York, to meet with the attorney. Court costs were later included. He was aware of the downside of his action. He said he knew there was a possibility he would be suspended from baseball, but he wasn't asking the Players Association for any remuneration. In fact, he agreed to pledge in writing that if he won any damages in the case, he would reimburse the Players Association for all out-of-pocket expenses.

It was a wide-open discussion. The members of the board and the player representatives were impressed with Flood's commitment and his determination to see this suit through to its conclusion. Curt encouraged those in attendance at the meeting to ask him anything they wanted to, and he answered everything in a straightforward fashion.

"From the beginning, I never doubted Curt's sincerity one bit. What a courageous thing he did."

From the beginning, I never doubted Curt's sincerity one bit. What a courageous thing he did. The money he gave up.

He had made $90,000 in 1969 and the Phillies, eager to sign him, offered him a raise of $10,000. Flood remained adamant and refused to sign. Spring training started and Flood didn't report, but the Phillies still didn't believe he was going to go through with his plan. During spring training, Phillies general manager John Quinn met with Flood over dinner in Philadelphia and upped the offer to Flood to a salary of $110,000 a year for five years. In those days, that was a ton of money, and I'm sure there were a lot of people who thought Flood was just calling their bluff, that he would cave in for more money. He never did.

Flood sat out the entire 1970 season. Eventually, the Phillies traded him to Washington, and Curt agreed to go there provided Marvin Miller assured him that it would not prejudice his case. Miller said it wouldn't, just as long as he was not playing in Philadelphia.

Flood reported to Washington, but he was 33 years old, and sitting out a year had eroded his skills. He played in 13 games with the Senators and was hitting just .200 when he decided he couldn't perform up to his usual standard any longer and retired. He left baseball and, except for doing some broadcasting in Oakland for a while, pretty much dropped out of sight.

Flood lost his case in Federal District Court and in the United States Court of Appeals. He then took his case to the ultimate and final arbiter, the United States Supreme Court, and lost again. But his courageous stand set in motion the wheels that would eventually lead to free agency—and the escalation of players' salaries—as we know it today.

Curt was very sensitive, a man with an artistic bent who was a talented portrait artist. He also had a wonderful, dry sense of humor. He was so clever. Get him together with Bob Gibson and the two of them would go at one

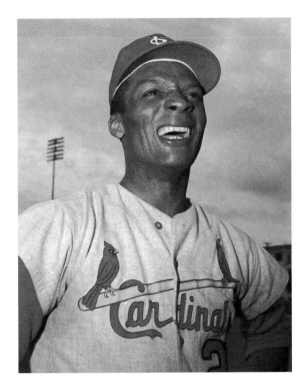

Curt Flood was a brilliant center fielder for the Cardinals, but his legacy to baseball is as the man who challenged the game's hallowed reserve clause. His courage and determination began the process of creating free agency—and is what allows players to earn the huge salaries they command today. *AP/Wide World Photos*

another in a way that would make you burst your sides laughing. They were hilarious together.

Flood and I had this ritual. We would pair off and play catch to warm up before the second game of doubleheaders. One day, between games, we were sitting in the dugout and the Southern University marching band was entertaining on the field at old Busch Stadium. I was amazed at their performance and by their athleticism. They had this routine where they would march and play and twirl their instruments all at the same time. It was a remarkable show.

I turned to Curt with this look of wonder on my face, and he just looked at me and said, "I know what you're thinking. Forget it. They're from the old country."

Because of his decision to challenge baseball's reserve clause, which led to subsequent landmark changes in the game, and his critical role in the history of baseball, there's a tendency to overlook Flood as a player. That's unfortunate. Curt, who is second on my all-time list, was a terrific player and an important part of our three championship teams in the sixties.

Curt was born in Houston, but he grew up in Oakland and signed with the Cincinnati Reds. The Cardinals got him as a throw-in in a relatively minor trade after the 1957 season. Getting Flood was an important part of assembling the teams that would be so successful in the sixties. The Cards had tried Ken Boyer in center field in 1957, but he was much better suited for third base, and when Flood arrived, Flood took over as the regular center fielder and the Cardinals moved Boyer back to third.

When Lou Brock came from the Cubs to the Cardinals and became our leadoff hitter, Flood was the perfect guy to bat behind him in the second spot. He was patient at the plate, which gave Brock the opportunity to use his great speed and steal all those bases. Curt could go deep in the count, hit behind the runner, and steal a base, and he was consistently in the .290 to .300 range. Don Drysdale called him the toughest out in the National League.

"Curt could go deep in the count, hit behind the runner, and steal a base, and he was consistently in the .290 to .300 range. Don Drysdale called him the toughest out in the National League."

Except for his arm, Flood was regarded as the equal of the great Willie Mays in center field. That's why it was such a shock, so uncharacteristic of Flood, that he misjudged a ball in center field during Game 7 of the 1968 World Series. Two runs scored and people say that play cost us the game. In reality, it was the left-handed effectiveness of Mickey Lolich that was the difference.

Gibson and Lolich, both of whom had pitched two complete-game victories in the Series, were hooked up in a pitchers' duel in Game 7. Going into the top of the seventh, the game was scoreless, but we felt we were in command. We had Gibson, our unbeatable ace, while Lolich was pitching with two days' rest.

Gibson had breezed through the first six innings. He was his usual overpowering, dominant self as he retired 18 of 19 batters, 6 of them on strikeouts. The only hit off him was Mickey Stanley's slow roller to short with one out in the fifth.

In the seventh inning, Gibby picked right up where he had left off. He struck out Stanley looking and got Al Kaline on a grounder to third. Then disaster struck. Norm Cash and Willie Horton hit back-to-back singles, bringing up Jim Northrup, a left-handed hitter, who hit a line drive to deep center. Just then, Flood got his feet lodged in the mud, causing him to misjudge the ball. It sailed over his head for a two-run triple. Bill Freehan doubled home Northrup, and the Tigers had scored three runs. Instead of going into the bottom of the seventh still at 0–0, we were down three, and those three runs seemed to energize Lolich. He finished up and beat us, 4–1, depriving the Cardinals of a second straight world championship. On a dry field, there's no doubt Curt would have sucked up Jim Northrup's seventh-inning drive.

After the 1981 season, the Cardinals and the Yankees made an obscure trade in which the Cards sent left-hander Bob Sykes to New York for a minor league outfielder named **Willie McGee**. Sykes never played a game in a Yankees uniform. In fact, he never played another major league game. McGee, who ranks third on my list, went on to have a distinguished 18-year career, 13 of them with the Cardinals, during which he was the league's Most Valuable Player, made the Cards' top 10 list in five offensive categories, and won

After Stan Musial, no Cardinal has been more popular than Willie McGee. *Lew Portnoy, Spectra-Action, Inc.*

two batting titles, one in 1985 and another in 1990, even though he was traded to Oakland late in the season.

Willie was the Cardinals' most popular contemporary player as fans connected with his gentility and humility as well as admiring his exciting style of play.

Jim Edmonds made such an immediate impact with the Cardinals after coming to them from the Anaheim Angels in the spring of 2000, he deserves a place on their all-time team after only three seasons in St. Louis. He's an acrobatic center fielder as well as a devastating power hitter, who may have been aided by being in the same lineup as Mark McGwire. But even without Big Mac, Edmonds continued to be an offensive force for the Cardinals. Edmonds is my pick for the number four spot.

Like Stan Musial, **Pepper Martin** was good enough to be listed in two positions, a rare tandem of third base and center field. He started out with the Cardinals in the outfield. He was their third baseman in 1933, 1934, when they won the World Series, and 1935. Then he returned to the outfield. I rate him fifth among Cardinals at both positions.

Bill Virdon would be on this list were it not for a myopic trade by Frank Lane, who was known as "Trader Lane" for good reason. It seemed Lane never saw a player on another team who he didn't like and didn't want to get. He had this compulsion to make trades, any trade, any time, often without considering the consequences.

Virdon had come through the Yankees farm system in the fifties, which at the time was loaded with outstanding young prospects that the Yankees used as so many chips to pick up pennant insurance. Jackie Jensen, Jim Greengrass, Norm Siebern, Lew Burdette, Bob Porterfield, and Vic Power are some of the people the Yankees traded away who became good players elsewhere.

The Cardinals got Virdon at the start of the 1954 season in the deal that sent Enos Slaughter to New York. Bill hardly had a chance to prove himself in St. Louis when, two years later, Lane sent him to Pittsburgh for outfielder Bobby Del Greco and a left-handed pitcher, Dick Littlefield, neither of whom did much to help the Cardinals. Lane had seen Del Greco hit three home runs in a game and decided right then that this was a player he had to have. He based the trade on that one game and got rid of someone who would have been a very productive player for the Cardinals for many years.

Virdon, an excellent defensive center fielder and leadoff hitter, ended up having an outstanding career in Pittsburgh. He played on the Pirates' 1960 World Series champion team, later was a division-winning manager with both the Pirates and the Astros, and would be included on any list of top five Pirates center fielders.

Jim Edmonds, who came to the Cardinals from the Angels in 2000, is known not only for his long-ball power, but also for his acrobatic catches in center field. *AP/Wide World Photos*

Statistical Summaries

All statistics are for player's Cardinals career only.

HITTING

G = Games

H = Hits

HR = Home runs

RBI = Runs batted in

SB = Stolen bases

BA = Batting average

Center Fielder	Years	G	H	HR	RBI	SB	BA
Terry Moore *Went six-for-six on September 5, 1935*	1935–42 1946–48	1,298	1,318	80	513	82	.280
Willie McGee *Had 10 hits in 1987 World Series vs. Minnesota*	1982–90 1996–99	1,661	1,683	63	678	301	.294
Curt Flood *Won seven consecutive Gold Gloves from 1963–69*	1958–69	1,738	1,853	84	633	88	.293

(continued)	Years	G	H	HR	RBI	SB	BA
Jim Edmonds *Hit 42 homers in his first season with Cards (2000)*	2000–2002	446	455	100	301	19	.303
Pepper Martin *Had hitting streaks of 24 and 23 games in 1935*	1928 1930–40 1944	1,189	1,227	59	501	146	.298

FIELDING

PO = Put-outs

A = Assists

E = Errors

DP = Double plays

TC/G = Total chances divided by games played

FA = Fielding average

Center Fielder	PO	A	E	DP	TC/G	FA
Terry Moore	3,117	102	48	23	2.7	.984
Willie McGee	3,282	93	86	19	2.4	.975
Curt Flood	4,005	114	53	28	2.5	.987
Jim Edmonds	1,009	32	15	7	2.4	.986
Pepper Martin	1,299	59	37	14	2.3	.973

EIGHT

Right Fielder

I HAVE THIS DILEMMA. Do I put **Stan Musial** at the top of the list of all-time Cardinals left fielders or at the top of the list of all-time Cardinals right fielders? He played both positions about an equal amount of the time. He even was their regular first baseman from 1956 through 1958, when Bill White came along, but most people regard Musial as an outfielder, either right or left.

Funny how Musial jumped back and forth between right field and left, usually switching with Enos "Country" Slaughter. I can't say for sure why they switched, but Slaughter was in right when Musial came up, so they put Stan in left. Then when Slaughter was in the service during World War II, Musial took his position in right field. In fairness, Stan was better suited to left field because of a poor throwing arm, and Slaughter had a strong right-fielder's arm. But Musial has said he liked right field better because it's a more natural position for a left-handed thrower like him. In left field, he often had to throw across his body.

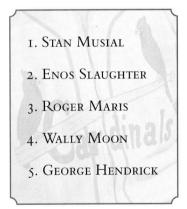

1. STAN MUSIAL

2. ENOS SLAUGHTER

3. ROGER MARIS

4. WALLY MOON

5. GEORGE HENDRICK

Because he was such a great hitter, Stan never gets the credit he deserves as a fly chaser, although, as I said, his throwing arm was suspect. As a young

How good was Stan Musial? Good enough to be rated number one on my all-time Cardinals team at two positions: left field and right field. As a young player, he had great speed and often played center field. *AP/Wide World Photos*

man, he had great speed and often played center field. As a right fielder, he was exceptional in getting to the ball, but his one weakness surfaced on the longer outfield throws, from right field to third base or home.

When Slaughter returned in 1946, he went back to right, Musial played first base, and Erv Dusak was in left. The following year, it was Musial at first, Dusak in right, Slaughter in left.

Slaughter offered the following explanation for his switch from right field to left. "In 1947, we wanted another left-handed hitter, so we got Ron

Northey from the Phillies [in a trade for Harry the "Hat" Walker]. Northey couldn't play left field. He always played right with the Phillies, so the manager, Eddie Dyer, asked me to go to left and I did."

Northey stayed with the Cardinals through the 1949 season, and then he was traded to Cincinnati, again in a deal for Harry Walker. With Northey gone, Slaughter returned to right field and stayed there until he was traded to the Yankees in 1954. Got it?

All that switching is confusing, and curious, but I solved the problem by making Musial number one in both left field and right. After all, he is Stan the Man, the greatest Cardinal of them all.

Enos Slaughter is number two. He had an excellent throwing arm, much better than Stan's, and he was a terrific outfielder and a solid hitter. Slaughter wasn't a big man, only 5′9″, 180 pounds, and he didn't hit a lot of home runs (never 20 in any season), but he was a good contact hitter, a line drive type, and a big run producer. He led the league in RBIs in 1946.

Slaughter was an anachronism, a player who was out of place in time. He should have been a member of the Gashouse Gang. That's the type of player he was: the quintessential hustler who ran everything out.

Legend has it that when he was a young player in the Cardinals farm system, Slaughter was reprimanded by his manager, Eddie Dyer, for failing to hustle. He vowed then and there never to be seen walking on a ball field. And he never was.

Slaughter earned his everlasting reputation for hustle for one play, on baseball's biggest stage, the World Series. It was in St. Louis in the seventh game of the 1946 Series between the Cardinals and the Red Sox.

The score was tied, 3–3, when Slaughter led off the bottom of the eighth with a single to center. The next two Cardinals made outs, and Enos was still on first with two outs when Harry Walker lined a hit over short. It looked like it might be just a routine single that would put Cardinals on first and third, maybe even first and second, or a short double, at best. In fact, it was scored a double, but, even with two outs and Slaughter running on the hit, it didn't appear there was any chance he could score.

Slaughter, off with the crack of the bat, wheeled around into third, where everybody expected him to stop, including Red Sox shortstop Johnny Pesky. But Enos never stopped running. He tore around third, through coach Mike Gonzalez's stop sign, and dashed home. Thinking Slaughter would stop at

Enos "Country" Slaughter was an anachronism. He was a star with the Cardinals in the forties, but his aggressive style was right out of the pages of the "Gashouse Gang's" manual. *AP/Wide World Photos*

third, Pesky hesitated just long enough that his throw home was too late to get Enos, who scored what proved to be the winning run of the World Series. That one play defined Slaughter's entire career and has stayed with him all these years as his legacy to the hell-bent-for-leather brand of baseball.

After he left the Cardinals, Slaughter became a pinch hitter deluxe for the Yankees' championship teams in 1956, 1957, and 1958. Eventually, he was inducted into the Hall of Fame. He died in August 2002 at the age of 86.

One of the most misunderstood, and most underrated, ballplayers of his time—maybe of all time—was **Roger Maris**. I know it sounds strange to call a player who broke Babe Ruth's cherished single-season home-run record underrated. The fact is, because he hit 61 home runs in 1961, one more than Ruth had hit in 1927, Maris was perceived as a one-dimensional player. Somewhere along the line, he also picked up the reputation of being surly and uncommunicative.

I found out firsthand that Roger, third on my list of all-time Cardinals right fielders, was anything but a one-dimensional ballplayer, and he was hardly surly or uncommunicative. He was a good guy with a sense of humor, and an outstanding all-around ballplayer who could hit, run, field, and throw. He had extraordinary baseball instincts.

I remember watching the 1962 World Series between the Yankees and the San Francisco Giants when Maris made one of the greatest plays I've ever seen by an outfielder. It was a game-saving, Series-saving play that typified those extraordinary instincts I mentioned.

It came in the bottom of the ninth inning with the Yankees leading, 1–0, with two outs and a runner on first. Willie Mays ripped one into the right-field corner that looked, when it left the bat, like a triple that would score Matty Alou from first with the tying run and leave the winning run 90 feet from home plate.

Reacting instinctively, Maris raced to his left and grabbed the ball, preventing it from rattling around the corner, and came up throwing a perfect strike to the cutoff man, second baseman Bobby Richardson, which held Alou, the tying run, on third. Willie McCovey then hit a line drive to Richardson to end the game and the Series. Ralph Terry was the hero of the World Series for winning Game 5 and then pitching a four-hitter to win Game 7, 1–0. Terry pitched a complete game, but Roger Maris deserved a save.

Five years after he sat on top of the world as baseball's all-time single-season home-run king, Maris was persona non grata in New York. His batting average plummeted to the .230s. He had hit only 21 homers in two seasons. He complained of a sore hand, but x-rays showed no apparent damage and some people accused Maris of jaking. To know Roger is to know that was ridiculous.

After the 1966 season, Maris was traded to the Cardinals for journeyman third baseman Charlie Smith. I will admit that when he came to us, most of the players were suspicious and curious. Were we wrong! Maris was a terrific teammate. He wasn't the player he once was, and he was used mostly against right-handed pitchers, but he brought with him those great instincts, his experience, and the influence of a winner. Before his two years with the Cardinals were up, he was looked up to like he never was with the Yankees.

He was the missing piece to the puzzle that helped us win the pennant by 10½ games over the Giants, then beat the Red Sox in seven games in the 1967 World Series.

Maris, who was devoted to his family, had stated that the 1967 season was going to be his last. He would retire and enjoy his time watching his children grow up. After his contributions helped us win the pennant, the Cardinals tried to talk him into playing one more year. Roger was reluctant, but the Cardinals were being very persuasive. Gussie Busch, the Cards' owner and the president of the Anheuser-Busch Brewery, promised Maris that if he would play in 1968, he would give Roger a Budweiser distributorship that would set up him and his family for life.

"See about it, my ass. Either it's in the contract or I'm not playing."

—Roger Maris

Inadvertently, I found out about this arrangement firsthand.

We had clinched the 1967 National League pennant in Philadelphia with two weeks left in the season, and the Cardinals had a victory party in a famous Philadelphia restaurant, Bookbinder's, after a night game. I arrived at the restaurant with John "Honey" Romano, a veteran catcher we had picked up over the winter from the White Sox.

When the evening's business was done, Romano and I were standing at the bar having a drink and within earshot were Maris and Gussie Busch. It soon became apparent to us that they were talking contract. We heard Maris say something about a beer distributorship.

Despite breaking Babe Ruth's home-run record when he hit 61 for the Yankees in 1961, Roger Maris (left) was one of the most unappreciated and misunderstood players ever. He was a Cardinal for two seasons, 1967 and 1968, and not only did he help us win two pennants and one World Series, he was a terrific teammate. Here Roger poses with Red Sox manager Dick Williams during the 1967 World Series. *AP/Wide World Photos*

"You hit 30 home runs and drive in 100 runs next season," Busch boomed, "and we'll see about it."

"See about it, my ass," Maris said. "Either it's in the contract or I'm not playing."

I looked at Romano and he looked at me and we both decided this was none of our business, so we moved to the other end of the bar. But that was the deal. Maris played the 1968 season and was influential in helping us win another pennant, then retired to his beer distributorship in Gainesville, Florida. He was only 34.

Wally Moon homered in his first at-bat in the major leagues. Remarkably, he beat out Henry Aaron for National League Rookie of the Year honors in 1954. It was an auspicious start for what the Cardinals thought would be a great career. Moon was being touted as the next Stan Musial. That might have been too much for any player to live up to and Moon never reached such lofty heights, but he did have four solid years with the Cards, and so I place him fourth on my list.

When his numbers fell off in 1958, Moon was traded to the Dodgers for Gino Cimoli. At the time, the Dodgers were using a temporary facility, the Los Angeles Coliseum, while awaiting the construction of Dodger Stadium. The Coliseum was ostensibly a football stadium. For baseball, they had erected a tall screen in left field where it measured only 250 feet down the line.

Moon gained a measure of fame for his ability to hit the ball over that left-field fence. A left-handed hitter, he perfected the inside-out swing that allowed him to pop inside pitches to left field and over that short fence. He hit 19 home runs for the Dodgers that year, many of them over the short left-field fence, which reporters referred to as "Moon shots," a feat equaled 10 years later by Neil Armstrong.

To fill out my top five right fielders, there are several choices. There's Chick Hafey and Pepper Martin, both of whom played some right field but who have been selected at other positions. Mike Shannon and Reggie Smith are also possibilities; Ernie Orsatti, a diminutive left-handed hitter who played mostly center field for the Gashouse Gang, was a lifetime .300 hitter and an intriguing character who had been a football player, a professional boxer, and an auto racer. He was also a Hollywood stunt man and stand-in for the famous silent-movie comedian and mime Buster Keaton.

After his first four years, Mike Shannon, another contender for fifth, appeared to be on the fast track to a place among Cardinals all-time right fielders. When we got Maris in 1967, Shannon, the consummate team player, was asked to switch to third base, a position he had never played. Not only did he make the switch, but he also worked hard to make himself into a better than adequate third baseman, good enough to play the position for two pennant winners. He was a tremendous competitor and a valuable member of those championship teams. Mike's career was cut short by nephritis, a serious kidney ailment. He became another Cardinal who went into the

A decade before Neil Armstrong, Wally Moon perfected the "Moon shot"—home runs over the left-field fence in the Los Angeles Coliseum with an inside-out swing—when he played for the Dodgers. *AP/Wide World Photos*

broadcast booth and has been a very popular Cardinals announcer for the past three decades.

Reggie Smith was a Cardinal for only two-and-a-half seasons, but he produced enough in that short time to be given serious consideration for my all-time list of Cardinals right fielders. Despite his short stint in St. Louis, it's hard to overlook Smith. His body of work with three teams over four decades, the fifties, sixties, seventies, and eighties—a near .300 hitter, a consistent 25-home-run guy, and a player who would drive in 80 to 100 runs a year—stamps him as one of the game's best switch-hitters.

However, my choice for number five among all-time Cardinals right fielders is **George Hendrick**, which may be surprising to some for a couple of reasons. George played for six teams in an 18-year career and was often overshadowed by more famous teammates, including Reggie Jackson in Oakland, Boog Powell and Buddy Bell in Cleveland, Dave Winfield in San Diego, and Keith Hernandez and Ted Simmons in St. Louis. And he was largely overlooked and underrated because of his refusal to speak to the press. A player who is uncooperative with the press suffers in that he will not get those lengthy laudatory articles written about him that help him get the recognition he deserves.

Hendrick never cared about recognition, and while he never was a media darling, he was a favorite of Cardinals fans and very popular with his teammates.

Hendrick came to the Cardinals in 1978 in a trade for pitcher Eric Rasmussen (put that down as another of the great trades in Cards history). In 102 games with the Cardinals that season, George hit 17 homers, drove in 67 runs, and batted .288. In three seasons, 1980, 1982, and 1983, he averaged 20 homers and 103 RBIs.

You'll notice I omitted the 1981 season. That was the year of the strike and might have been George's best with the Cards. In 101 games, he led the Cardinals in slugging percentage, runs, total bases, RBIs, and extra base hits.

Not only was Hendrick a devastating hitter, but he was a superb fielder with a strong throwing arm as well. He committed only two errors in each of the 1979 and 1980 seasons. After Hernandez was traded to the Mets in 1983, Hendrick filled in at first base and did a more than adequate job there in 92 games.

When Cardinals fans talk about the 1982 World Series victory over the Milwaukee Brewers, they'll invariably mention Hernandez, Willie McGee,

Darrell Porter, and Bruce Sutter. Once again, George Hendrick gets over-looked, but he tied Lonnie Smith for the team lead in batting at .321, drove in five runs, and led the team in on-base percentage. And it was Hendrick's RBI single in the bottom of the sixth that capped a three-run rally and put the Cardinals ahead to stay in the seventh game.

Even in leaving St. Louis, Hendrick made a tremendous contribution to the Cardinals. When he was sent to Pittsburgh after the 1984 season, the player the Cards got in return was John Tudor.

His adversarial relationship with the press prevented George Hendrick from getting the recognition he deserved, but his teammates and the St. Louis fans loved him. *Lew Portnoy, Spectra-Action, Inc.*

NINE

Right-Handed Pitcher

YOU DON'T NEED ME to tell you about **Bob Gibson**'s greatness as a pitcher, but I will. Go to the record books and check him out: the 251 wins, the 3,117 strikeouts, the record 1.12 earned run average, 13 shutouts and 28 complete games in 1968, the record 17 strikeouts in one game, and a 7–2 mark in the World Series, including seven straight wins.

All impressive numbers, to be sure, but they're only numbers, and they come nowhere near to telling the full story of Bob Gibson, who tops my list.

I can't talk about Gibson without mentioning two things: his extraordinary ability fueled by a compelling personality and intelligence; and his fire, drive, and tenacity. Bob is second to Stan Musial in Cardinals lore, a warrior and a gladiator, who, if he lived during the Roman Empire, would have been the only one victorious over the lions. Russell Crowe he was.

1. BOB GIBSON

2. JESSE HAINES

3. DIZZY DEAN

4. MORT COOPER

5. BOB FORSCH

To me, Gibson is a dichotomy, a man with a relentless competitive drive and one of the warmest, most compassionate people I've ever known. Bob is a complex individual. His gruff exterior belies a very warm interior. Those

119

who know him only casually, or through what they saw of him on the ball field, will never believe that. And Bob himself would cringe at that description. But his friends will attest to his warmth. Bob's friends are Bob's friends. They would do anything for him and they know he would do anything for them.

As a pitcher, Gibson was an artist, a perfectionist, and a tyrant, malicious and unyielding. It was his pitcher's mound and nobody else was welcome on it, as I found out many times.

Gibby was an awesome, overpowering, dominant pitcher, especially in the 1967 and 1968 seasons. There was nothing he couldn't do. His ball always exploded, but in those years he mastered the outside corner on right-handed hitters. Occasionally, he had trouble with left-handed hitters. Ron Fairly hit him well. Ken Boswell and Dave Marshall of the Mets and Willie McCovey of the Giants were tough outs for him. But I always felt he could throw any pitch at any time to a right-handed hitter with William Tell accuracy. He could thread a needle . . . or an apple. He could throw the ball within two baseball widths of the outside corner, with movement and at 95 miles an hour. I never caught anybody else like that.

There was a tendency, if you were catching him, to fall into a stupor and just become a fan. I was taking part in history, and the only thing that saved me was that he worked so fast and was so difficult to catch, he never gave me a chance to fall into an enraptured state.

His 1968 season, the 1.12 ERA, was simply staggering. He pitched 13 shutouts, won 15 straight games, and had one stretch of 95 consecutive innings in which he allowed just two runs, only one of them earned. He struck out 268 batters that season and walked only 62, a strikeout-to-walk ratio of almost 5 to 1. It's amazing that he lost nine games, but he lost five of them by the score of 1–0.

One of those 1–0 games was against the Pirates in Forbes Field. After the game, I went up to him in the clubhouse and patted him on the back.

"Helluva game," I said.

Gibson exploded as only he could. "Helluva game, my ass. You guys can't score one run?"

I just slinked away. Later, I was in the shower room shaving. He moved in next to me and started to shave. After a few seconds, Bob looked over and said, "Hey, about that thing before . . ."

I understood it to be his way of apologizing for jumping all over me earlier. No apology was necessary. It *never* and *always* was personal with Gibson. Bob was Bob.

When Gibson went off on one of his tirades, you could take one of two routes. You could shrink like a 10-day-old rose or stand up to him, be counted, and enjoy. Fortunately, the Cardinals had guys who responded very well to him.

In 1968, when he was in the midst of that great season, we were in San Francisco and we were leading, 5–0. Jim Ray Hart led off the bottom of the eighth with a triple, so the Giants had a runner on third, no outs, and Mays and McCovey coming up. But we were obviously still in control of the game.

"Ball back to you," I shouted to Gibson. "You're going to first."

"No, I'm not," he said. "I'm coming home."

"Dammit, Bob," I said, "that makes no sense. We've got a five-run lead. Get the out."

"No," he shouted. "He's not scoring."

And Hart didn't score. Gibson knew he was in the midst of something special. He had a chance to be the best ever and he realized that.

I must have had hundreds of run-ins with Gibson over the early years, some business-related, some personal, but all unforgettable. The thing about Gibson is that you couldn't be sensitive; he'd run all over you. If you were overly sensitive, he'd come at you full force. He was teaching you, educating you to toughness.

I'd go out to the mound if he was in trouble, and he'd glower at me and begin yelling, "Tim, what the ★&^%$! are you doing out here? The only thing you know about pitching is that it's tough to hit." It's a line often heard in baseball.

Part of me would be mad at him and the other part of me would be laughing. Then, after the game, I'd get mad for a minute, and then I'd start laughing again.

When he was the manager of the Cardinals, Johnny Keane would always complain that Gibson worked too fast, and he would get on me to slow him down. I'd say to John, "If you want to slow him down, *you* go out there. I've been out there too many times and, like tithing, I've already given. I refuse to be a punching bag for him."

My teammate, my friend, and the greatest competitor I ever saw on a baseball field, Bob Gibson has intelligence and wit and is the most brutally honest person I know. Oh, yes, he also was a pretty damn good pitcher. *AP/Wide World Photos*

122

You always knew that if Gibson was pitching, the chance of something unsettling happening was great.

In 1965, Red Schoendienst took over as manager of the Cardinals, and in the first game of the year, Gibson was pitching against the Cubs at Wrigley Field and he was getting hit pretty hard. So, Red went to the mound to take Gibby out of the game, and Gibson started yelling at Red. I was in the bullpen, recovering from a broken finger, and I could hear Gibson screaming all the way out there. "Dammit, Red, this isn't the World Series. It's Opening Day."

Red didn't know what to do. After that, he'd send his pitching coach out to talk to Gibson. Nobody wanted to go to the mound when Gibson was pitching. When Barney Schultz was the pitching coach, he would go to the mound and Gibson would shout at him, "Barney, what are you going to tell me? You threw a knuckleball. I don't throw a knuckleball."

We were playing a doubleheader in Philadelphia in 1973, and Bob met up with Bill Cosby, a good friend of his. Cosby had his two sons at the game and the plan, since Bob was pitching the first game, was for Bill and his sons to come to the clubhouse to get together with Bob and then go out. That day, the Phillies teed off on Gibson. We were in the third inning and losing, 8–2, when here comes Barney Schultz to the mound to take Gibson out of the game. I was playing first base, Ted Simmons was catching, and Joe Torre was playing third. The three of us assembled on the mound waiting for Schultz to get out there.

It took Barney forever to go from the dugout to the mound. He was walking slowly, his head down, expecting Gibson to explode. But when Barney was within hearing range, Bob exploded playfully.

"Barney, where the ★&$%^@! have you been? I've been getting my ass kicked. What took you so long?"

Then Gibson just handed the ball to Schultz and calmly walked off the mound, and Torre, Simmons, and I were laughing like crazy. Even Barney had to laugh.

We knew Cosby was coming to the clubhouse after the game, so Torre intercepted Bill and told him to give Gibson some time. But because he was so congenial to Schultz, we figured him to be in pretty good humor despite getting belted around by the Phillies. Cosby came in and said something to Gibson, and Bob treated him as apathetically as some fan who had just come in off the street.

Bill just said, "I shoulda known better than to come in here after Bob lost a game."

That's the thing about Bob. He's not going to be any different toward you just because you're a friend or a celebrity. He's going to say exactly what's on his mind. Of all his traits, and he has many, the one that stands out is honesty. He could never be a phony. He didn't suffer fools easily.

In 1969, when President Richard Nixon entertained the All-Star teams at the White House, the All-Stars lined up in a receiving line to shake Nixon's hand. The only one who didn't was Bob Gibson. He didn't like Nixon and he wasn't going to be a hypocrite and shake his hand, White House or no White House.

If Stan Musial was the greatest Cardinal of them all, Bob Gibson was not far behind. His passion, his drive, and his desire to succeed were infectious. He inspired his teammates to be just as demanding, just as competitive, and just as hungry to succeed as he was. Almost.

Gibson was a role model for younger Cardinals, an enormous influence on others, such as Steve Carlton.

"I think Steve will tell you I influenced him," said Gibson. "It was not a conscious thing. He just watched me. I didn't coach him or anything. If I had an influence on him, it was that he studied my approach to the game and tried to copy it."

Gibson isn't among those who condemn the Cardinals for trading Carlton to the Phillies for Rick Wise.

"Steve had a lot of potential, you could see that," Gibson said. "But he was just one of a few young pitchers the Cardinals had at the time who had potential. There was Mike Torrez and Jerry Reuss and Carlton. You never know when that potential is going to blossom. To me, the trade wasn't that big a deal. Not what it turned out to be.

"You can't second-guess the Cardinals for making the trade. Rick Wise was a veteran pitcher who was a proven winner, and Carlton was still a prospect, even though he had won 20 games the year before. Teams are always trading away prospects and sometimes it comes back to haunt them. The Cardinals almost traded me and Joe Cunningham to Washington, but the Senators turned down the deal."

Gibson's competitiveness was never more evident than in the 1967 season. On July 15, a line drive off the bat of Roberto Clemente smashed into his right leg, just above the ankle. He shook off the pain and continued in the game for one more batter, but the leg was broken. It would sideline Gibson for two months.

Before he was injured, Gibson had a record of 10–6 and the Cardinals were in contention for the National League pennant. Amazingly, from the beginning of the season until the September 1 call-ups, the Cardinals made only one roster change. When Gibson went down, they traded Al Jackson to the Mets for Jack Lamabe, but it was Nelson Briles who carried the Cards in Gibson's absence. Briles was especially brilliant, finishing the season with 11 wins in his last 12 decisions.

There were some who believed Gibson felt his importance to the Cardinals was minimized as the Cardinals continued to win without him. The thought never entered Gibson's mind.

"I've never been the kind of person who was insecure about my ability and what I could accomplish," Gibson said. "I couldn't stand not playing. That was driving me crazy. I was too busy feeling sorry for myself to think about the team winning without me. But I was happy they were winning. I wanted another chance to pitch in the World Series."

Gibson would get that chance. He returned in September, won three and lost one, pitched the pennant clincher in Philadelphia, and was the starting pitcher for the Cardinals in Game 1 of the 1967 World Series against the Boston Red Sox. He won the Series opener in Boston, 2–1. In Game 4, he pitched a five-hit shutout. Then in Game 7, Gibson pitched a three-hitter, struck out 10, hit a home run, and beat the Red Sox, 7–2. He was the first pitcher in 10 years to win three games in a World Series.

Gibson's reputation as an intimidator is legendary. Brushing guys back, knocking guys down, hitting guys—intentionally or otherwise—was the way pitchers operated then. When you had a reputation, every time you hit a batter, people thought you were throwing to hit him. In Jim Ray Hart's first major league game, Gibson broke his left shoulder with a pitch. In Tommie Agee's first spring training game with the Mets, Bob hit him in the head. He wasn't trying to hit either of them.

Don't get me wrong; he'd knock a hitter down and he'd pitch inside in a second, and he never allowed you the inside part of the plate. But I know that in those two famous incidents, he was trying to hit neither.

Pete Rose used to run across the mound when he made an out. It was his way of intimidating the pitcher, and it was very smart. It didn't work with Gibson. The mound was Gibby's office and he didn't let anyone into his office.

One day, Rose flied out, and as he turned first base and headed back to the dugout, he crossed right behind the mound. The next time Pete came to bat,

Gibson knocked him down. Pete got up and spit at Bob, and Bob threw the next pitch behind Rose. Pete didn't spit anymore.

In Dave Winfield's rookie year in San Diego, he hit a home run off Gibson and then glared at Gibby as he was running around the bases. The next time Winfield came to bat, you guessed it, Gibson leveled him. Winfield is a big man, and he went down in sections, all six feet, six inches of him, his legs going one way, his arms another.

To Dave's credit, he accepted it. He got up, dusted himself off, and must have thought, "I heard about this guy and what I heard was right."

When Roberto Clemente hit a line drive and broke Gibson's foot in 1967 (it happened in the first inning and Bob threw five more pitches with a broken foot), Clemente considered it justice because Gibson often knocked Roberto down. Clemente figured what goes around, comes around. Clemente used to tell Gibson, "If I were a pitcher and you were a hitter, how would you like it if I knocked you down?"

Gibson would just look at him with a smile and say, "Well, that's not the case, is it?"

When batters were hit then, compassion from a pitcher was rare. That's just the way the game was played back then, and Gibson played it better than anybody. He drove himself to be the best. He was compelled to do things the right way. His regimen between starts was as sharp as his performance, and he was as strict with himself as he was with others. He demanded as much from himself as he demanded from others. It became an obsession with him. He took care of his body, and his body rewarded him.

That desire to be the best extended beyond his pitching. He was a complete player, a guy who could beat you with the bat, with his legs, and with his glove, as well as with his arm. He hit 24 home runs in his career, and one year he batted over .300. Another year, he stole five bases. He won the Gold Glove for defense nine straight years.

Bob was an outstanding basketball player at Creighton University, and when he graduated, he played with the Harlem Globetrotters. The Trotters are famous for putting on a show with their ball-handling and other tricks. Bob apparently didn't go for that. He wanted to win, so he played it straight. More than once he had to be told, "Bob, Meadowlark Lemon is the star of this team."

When he signed with the Cardinals, they ordered him to give up playing basketball because they were afraid he'd get hurt. Gibby refused. He told the

Cardinals, "They're paying me $1,000 a month to play, and I need the money."

So, in the winter of 1958 and 1959, the Cardinals paid Gibson $4,000 *not* to play basketball.

Jack Buck, who was a Cardinals broadcaster for more than 50 years, and who was just as much the voice of the NFL for years, said that Gibson is "the best athlete I've ever seen. Nobody's close."

"Gibson has received every accolade imaginable, so much praise, so much admiration, all of it deserved."

Gibson was a man of rituals, and one of his best, and most hilarious, was his blackboard sessions at the end of the season. Every September, the whole team would gather around and Gibson would stand in front of a blackboard and determine the fate of every player on the roster. He'd have two columns. One was a list of players who were going to be traded, the other a list of players who were staying.

Nobody was immune to Gibson's barbs. He'd get rid of practically the whole team, including the manager. Invariably, the only two names on the list of players who were staying would be his own and Lou Brock's. Everybody else would be in the other column with some funny comment that was pure Gibson.

About me, he'd say, "McCarver's throws are fading between first and second. His throws are like skeet shooting. When you're shooting skeet, you yell, 'Pull.' When McCarver throws to second we yell, 'Pull.'"

One year, Gibson was into his blackboard act and suddenly there was a hush in the room. Bing Devine, our general manager, had walked into the room. Bing rarely came into the clubhouse and, though a fine man, he rarely laughed at anything. At first Gibson didn't see Devine, then he spotted him and, without missing a beat, he said, "Bing, I was going to get to you. You're gone, too."

Even Devine had to laugh.

Gibson has received every accolade imaginable, so much praise, so much admiration, all of it deserved. Something Johnny Keane once said stands as the definitive comment about him and is perhaps his ultimate tribute.

It was in the 1964 World Series against the Yankees. We won the first game, and then Mel Stottlemyre, a rookie, out-pitched Gibson to win Game 2. With three days' rest, Gibson pitched 10 innings and we won the fifth game, 5–2.

Gibson started Game 7 in St. Louis with just two days' rest. We broke a scoreless tie with three in the fourth, then scored three more in the fifth to lead, 6–0. But the Yankees came back with three in the top of the sixth when Mickey Mantle got Gibson for a three-run homer.

We picked up another run on Ken Boyer's home run in the seventh and went into the ninth leading 7–3, three outs away from the world championship. It was obvious Gibson was running out of gas. With one out, Clete Boyer hit a home run to make it 7–4. One out later, Phil Linz, a light-hitting infielder, also homered, and it was 7–5. Keane had Barney Schultz warming up in the bullpen, but he chose to stay with Gibson, whom he had managed in the minor leagues at Omaha.

Gibson was pitching on fumes, but he had enough stamina to get Bobby Richardson on a pop fly to second baseman Dal Maxvill.

After the game, when the writers asked Keane why he didn't bring in Schultz, what made him stay with Gibson, Johnny simply said, "I was committed to his heart."

I obviously never knew my number two choice, **Jesse Haines**, who pitched for the Cardinals from 1920 through 1937. Nor did I know anybody who knew him or saw him pitch. But when I read about Haines, it occurred to me he must have been the Bob Gibson of his day.

Haines played for the Cardinals longer than any other pitcher, 18 years, and pitched his entire career with the Cardinals except for one game with Cincinnati. Haines won 210 games, had three 20-win seasons, and pitched the Cardinals' first no-hitter of the 20th century. Only Gibson won more games and pitched more complete games for the Cardinals than Haines, and only Gibson, Dizzy Dean, and Bob Forsch struck out more batters for the Cardinals than Haines.

Apparently, Haines was a pleasant, mild-mannered man off the field, but on the field he was an intense competitor who would lose his temper with his teammates when poor defense cost him a game. Like Gibson, he also was an excellent hitter. In Game 3 of the 1926 World Series, Haines shut out the Yankees, 4–0, and hit a two-run home run.

That was the World Series that produced one of the great moments in baseball history. Haines started the seventh game and allowed only two runs through six innings. He developed a blister in the seventh and loaded the bases with two outs. In came the legendary Grover Cleveland Alexander,

From what I've read about Jesse Haines, he must have been the Bob Gibson of his day. With 210 career wins he was a fierce competitor on the field and a good hitter who pitched a shutout and hit a two-run home run against the Yankees in the third game of the 1926 World Series. *Bettman/CORBIS*

Jerome Herman, or Jay Hanna "Dizzy" Dean, the colorful Cardinals pitcher of the thirties, is the last pitcher to win 30 games (1934). When an arm injury shortened his career, he went into the broadcast booth and fractured the English language. *AP/Wide World Photos*

aging and at the end of his career, to strike out Tony Lazzeri and leave the bases loaded.

Haines was the winning pitcher, but Alexander was the hero of the game and his strikeout of Lazzeri was a highlight of the film about Alexander's life, *The Winning Team*. Ronald Reagan played Alexander. The role of Jesse Haines was played by former Cleveland Indians Hall of Famer and former Yankees manager Bob Lemon.

Late in his career, Haines developed a knuckleball, but with a twist. Most knuckleballers grip the baseball with their fingertips. Haines actually gripped it with his knuckles. The pitch allowed him to stay in the major leagues past his 44th birthday.

Dizzy Dean, who told some people his real name was Jerome Herman Dean and others that it was Jay Hanna Dean, was easily one of the most colorful characters in baseball history. Whatever his real name was, at his peak, Dean was an overpowering pitcher who won 102 games in a four-year period, from 1933 to 1936, and is the last National Leaguer to win 30 games in a season.

When his brother Paul (naturally, he was called "Daffy") joined the Cardinals in 1934, Dizzy proudly boasted that "me 'n Paul will win 45 games this year," even though the younger Dean had not yet won a game in the major leagues. The rookie won 19 and Dizzy won 30, exceeding Dean's prediction by 4.

Third on my list of all-time Cardinals right-handed pitchers, Dizzy might have gone on to even greater heights if it were not for an accident that shortened his career. Pitching in the 1937 All-Star Game, Dean suffered a broken toe when he was hit by a line drive off the bat of Earl Averill. Dizzy attempted to come back before the toe was completely healed. Favoring his injured toe, he altered his pitching motion and hurt his arm. He would never be the same again.

Before the start of the 1938 season, Dean was traded to the Cubs. With the Cardinals, he had won 134 games. He would win only 16 more for the remainder of his career.

When he was finished, Dizzy became a baseball broadcaster and enjoyed a 20-year career. With his malaprops and fractured grammar, Dizzy was as colorful behind the microphone as he was on the mound. If you heard the announcer say a player "slud" into second base, you knew you were listening to Dizzy Dean.

Mort Cooper is fourth on my list. Mort and Walker Cooper formed what many believe to be the best brother battery ever in baseball when they played for the Cardinals in the early forties. Mort was the ace of the staff for the Cardinals championship teams in 1942–43–44, winning 20 games each year.

In May of 1945, Cooper was traded to the Braves after he left the Cardinals in a salary dispute and was suspended, an act of spite that would be repeated by the penurious Cardinals several times over the next few decades.

Only two brothers have pitched no-hitters in the major leagues and they weren't the Deans. Dizzy never pitched a no-hitter; his brother, Paul, who won 100 fewer games than Diz, did.

Paul's feat happened in September 1934, in a doubleheader between the Cardinals and the Dodgers in Ebbets Field, Brooklyn. Dizzy pitched the first game and shut out the Dodgers on three hits. Paul pitched the second game and outdid his more famous, more skillful big brother by pitching a no-hitter.

Dizzy was proud of his kid brother's achievement, but he was also somewhat annoyed.

"That's real Dean pitchin'," he said. "But why didn't you tell me you was going to throw a no-hitter, 'cause I'da throwed one, too."

Bob Forsch and his brother Ken are the only brothers to have each "throwed" a no-hitter in the major leagues. Bob did it for the Cardinals on April 16, 1978, against the Phillies. Nine days short of one year later, Ken pitched a no-hitter for the Astros against the Braves.

Bob, my number five choice, would pitch another no-hitter for the Cards in 1983 and go on to win 168 games in a 16-year career, in addition to being one of the best hitting pitchers I've ever seen.

Some of the greatest pitchers in major league history have worn the uniform of the St. Louis Cardinals. I'm talking about Cy Young, Grover Cleveland Alexander, Kid Nichols, Vic Willis, Dazzy Vance, Mordecai "Three Finger" Brown, Pud Galvin, Burleigh Grimes, and Hoyt Wilhelm, all Hall of Famers. But they don't make my list of the all-time top five Cardinals right-handers because their time with the Cards was too brief.

The five-man rotation for the 1942 world champion Cardinals included two who make my all-time team: Mort Cooper in the center and Max Lanier on the left. The others are Ernie White, second from left, Johnny Beazley, fourth from left, and Harry Gunbert, right. Cooper won 22 games, Beazley 21. *Bettman/CORBIS*

Bob Forsch and his brother, Ken, are the only siblings to pitch no-hitters in the major leagues—Bob with the Cardinals in 1983 and Ken with the Astros the following year.
Lew Portnoy, Spectra-Action, Inc.

The Cardinals have a long list of outstanding right-handed pitchers and I would be remiss if I didn't mention Bill Doak, who won 20 games for the Cards in 1914 and 1920; Curt Davis from the thirties; George Munger from the forties; Larry Jackson from the fifties, one of the classiest people I met in the game; Joaquin Andujar, who had back-to-back 20-win seasons in the eighties; right up to the present day ace, Matt Morris.

Statistical Summaries

All statistics are for player's Cardinals career only.

PITCHING

G = Games

W = Games won

L = Games lost

PCT = Winning percentage

SHO = Shutouts

SO = Strikeouts

ERA = Earned run average

Right-Handed Pitcher	Years	G	W	L	PCT	SHO	SO	ERA
Bob Gibson *Won nine consecutive Gold Gloves from 1965–73*	1959–75	528	251	174	.591	56	3,117	2.91
Jesse Haines *Holds a 1.67 ERA in six career World Series games*	1920–37	554	210	158	.571	24	981	3.64
Dizzy Dean *First N.L. pitcher to win an All-Star Game (1936)*	1930 1932–37	273	134	75	.641	23	1,095	2.99

(continued)	Years	G	W	L	PCT	SHO	SO	ERA
Mort Cooper *Won 1942 N.L. MVP (22–7, 1.78 ERA)*	1938–45	228	105	50	.677	28	758	2.77
Bob Forsch *Led Cardinals pitchers in victories during six seasons*	1974–88	455	163	127	.562	19	780	3.67

FIELDING

PO = Put-outs

A = Assists

E = Errors

DP = Double plays

TC/G = Total chances divided by games played

FA = Fielding average

Right-Handed Pitcher	PO	A	E	DP	TC/G	FA
Bob Gibson	291	484	42	46	1.5	.949
Jesse Haines	106	650	27	32	1.4	.966
Dizzy Dean	64	241	14	15	1.2	.956
Mort Cooper	36	224	13	14	1.2	.952
Bob Forsch	220	393	17	34	1.4	.973

TEN

Left-Handed Pitcher

MY FIRST MEMORABLE EXPERIENCE with **Steve Carlton**, my number one left-handed pitcher, came during spring training 1965, in St. Petersburg, Florida. At the time, Carlton was a promising young left-hander trying to win a job on the big league team. He started one day, pitched the standard four innings, then left the game. Instead of doing his running, showering, dressing, and leaving, as pitchers do in spring training, Carlton waited until the game was over and I had returned to the clubhouse.

1. STEVE CARLTON

2. HARRY BRECHEEN

3. HOWIE POLLET

4. MAX LANIER

5. JOHN TUDOR

Carlton came over and confronted me awkwardly. "Tim," he said, "you've got to call for more breaking balls behind in the count."

I couldn't believe my ears. I had been in the big leagues for five years; the year before I was the catcher on a team that won the World Series, and here was this 20-year-old kid who hadn't even pitched in a major league game and he's criticizing my pitch selection. I let him have it in no uncertain terms. He just shrugged his shoulders and walked away.

That's Steve Carlton. He can be matter-of-factly obstinate and not know it. He even thinks it's funny—and it often is.

It was in the Hall of Fame exhibition game in Cooperstown in 1966 that Steve opened the Cardinals' eyes and made them realize they had a star in the making. He was a double-digit winner in each of the next four seasons and then exploded big time in 1971 when he won 20 games and lost only 9.

"That's Steve Carlton. He can be matter-of-factly obstinate and not know it. He even thinks it's funny—and it often is."

That winter, Carlton became involved in a bitter holdout with the Cardinals. He had made $55,000 in 1971 and was asking for a $10,000 raise, which the Cardinals refused to grant. Spring training had just started when the Cardinals, in what seemed like a fit of pique, traded Carlton to the Phillies for right-hander Rick Wise. Wise was a good pitcher, but he was no Steve Carlton. In fact, few, if any, were.

Although it was not perceived as such at first, that trade would turn out to be one of the worst in baseball history. For a lousy $10,000, the Cardinals traded away a guy who would win 251 games for the Phillies, become the second-winningest left-hander of all-time (behind Warren Spahn), the second leading strikeout pitcher in baseball history (behind Nolan Ryan), a four-time Cy Young Award winner, and a Hall of Famer. In the years Carlton was with the Phillies, the Cardinals finished second twice and third a bunch of times. Meanwhile the Phillies won five division titles, two pennants, and one World Series. I've often wondered how many more championships the Cardinals might have won if Carlton had not been traded.

Wise pitched for the Cardinals for two seasons and won 16 games each season, which is not bad. When he came to St. Louis and won his first five decisions, Cardinals fans actually thought they got the better of the deal. It wasn't long before they realized they were wrong. But here's where the Cardinals saved face in the Carlton-for-Wise deal. It's six degrees of separation.

After two years in St. Louis, Wise was traded for Reggie Smith, who was traded for Joe Ferguson, who was traded for Tony Scott, who was traded for Joaquin Andujar, one tough Dominican, who won 15 games during the regular season, beat the Braves in the third game of the National League Championship Series to clinch the pennant, then beat the Brewers in Game 3 and Game 7 of the 1982 World Series, just 10 years after the Carlton-for-Wise trade.

Here's the real irony of the Carlton-for-Wise trade. Rick also made $55,000 in 1971 and also was looking for a $10,000 raise, which is why the

I thought Steve Carlton was obstinate and brash when I first met him. He was 20 at the time. Twelve years later I was his personal catcher when he won 23 games for the Phillies. Seventeen years after that I was honored when Lefty invited me to be his guest at his installation into the Hall of Fame. *AP/Wide World Photos*

Phillies wanted to unload him. As it turned out, both Carlton and Wise eventually signed for $65,000, so these two pitchers who were traded for each other because of their salary demands both signed for what they wanted in the first place.

Another irony is that after getting off to such an awkward start with a young Carlton, I would end up being closely associated with him as his so-called personal catcher in Philadelphia. Here's how that happened.

I had been traded to the Phillies in 1970, then to Montreal, back to St. Louis, then to Boston. The Red Sox released me during the 1975 season and the Phillies brought me back. My role was to be a backup to their regular catcher, Bob Boone. I'd give Boonie a day off against some right-handed pitchers, catch the second game of doubleheaders, occasionally pinch hit.

Soon after I arrived in Philadelphia, we had a meeting that included team owner Ruly Carpenter, manager Danny Ozark, pitching coach Ray Rippelmeyer, and our three catchers, Bob Boone, Johnny Oates, and me. Carlton, or "Lefty" as we called him, was having his third straight subpar year and the Phillies were in a quandary. They had no idea what was wrong with him, and this meeting was to try to get to the bottom of the problem.

Everyone had his say about what he thought was wrong with Carlton. And everyone, except for Rippelmeyer and me, was convinced that he wasn't throwing his fastball enough.

At one point I said, "I'll probably get voted down here, but I played against Lefty and I played with him in St. Louis when he developed the slider, and, to me, he's not throwing the slider enough."

Only Rippelmeyer kind of agreed with me, but not vociferously. After the meeting, Ray came up to me and said, "You know, I've said that. He's not throwing the slider enough, and Boonie wants to keep setting hitters up with the fastball."

"If I ever catch him," I told Ray, "I'll call for his slider, I guarantee you that."

I had a chance to hit against his slider, and I'd also heard right-handed hitters come into the dugout and say, "He got me out, but at least he didn't throw me that slider."

When you hear comments like that from good right-handed hitters, it makes an impression. They know that slider's devastating, too. If they don't like to see it, it stands to reason Carlton should be throwing it more often.

As fate would have it, I got to catch Lefty some in 1975, and he was comfortable with me because I had caught him in St. Louis. In 1976, whenever Lefty pitched, I was his catcher, and you can bet I called for his slider a lot. I've kidded about it since. I said after catching so many of Carlton's sliders, I walked around for about four years shaking hands with three fingers.

When Lefty was elected to the Hall of Fame in 1994, he invited me to attend the induction ceremonies in Cooperstown, New York, as his guest.

It's the only time I've ever been to the Hall of Fame ceremonies, and it turned out to be one of the most memorable weekends of my life.

On the night before the induction ceremonies there's a private dinner party for Hall of Famers and guests of the inductees only. No media, no sponsors. After dinner, the new Hall of Famers get up to talk and anyone else who wants to speak can do so.

Carlton made a very nice, warm speech, thanking everybody who had been instrumental in his career, and when he was done, the emcee, George Grande of ESPN, asked me if I wanted to say something. I declined, but from my table I heard the unmistakable voice of Reggie Jackson. "You gotta get up and say something," he said so loud that everyone heard it, so there was nothing for me to do but speak.

They brought me a cordless mike. I said something like, "If Carl Hubbell is known for his screwball . . . and he was. And if Sandy Koufax is known for his curve ball . . . and he was. And if Nolan Ryan is the greatest strikeout pitcher of all time . . . and he is. Then Steve Carlton is the guy with the best slider ever thrown."

Then I said, "We love you, Lefty, and we're so proud of you."

When I was finished, I hugged him. While we were hugging, I could see over Lefty's shoulder a figure weaving his way through the emotional crowd. It was Bob Gibson. The next thing I knew, Gibby was four inches from my face, glaring into my eyes saying, "You mean the best *left-handed* slider you ever caught." Then he just skulked away as only Gibson can. Gibsonesque and hilarious.

I once made an offhand remark about Carlton. "When we die," I said, "we're going to be buried sixty feet, six inches apart." I was obviously kidding, but for some reason the remark was picked up and over the years I've seen it quoted many times.

In the forties and into the fifties, the Cardinals had four left-handed pitchers—Alpha Brazle, **Harry Brecheen**, Howard Pollet, and Max Lanier—who were effective and versatile. All four were used both as starters and relievers. In 1952, for example, Brazle led the league in saves and also started six games.

Of the four, Brecheen, who is second among all-time Cardinals left-handed pitchers, is probably the best known. He was called "Harry the Cat"

Harry the "Cat" Brecheen (right), second on my list of all-time Cardinals left-handed pitchers, with his batterymate Joe Garagiola (center), was one of the pioneers who went from the playing field to the broadcast booth. On the left is the third of three Boyer brothers who played in the major leagues, Cloyd, who pitched for the Cards from 1946 to 1952. *AP/Wide World Photos*

because of his agility on the mound and his ability as a fielder. He bounced around with catlike quickness, flagged down balls hit back to the box, and pounced on bunts and slow rollers. They had not yet begun awarding the Gold Glove for fielding excellence in Brecheen's day, but if they had, he would have dominated the award in the forties as Bobby Shantz did in the fifties and Jim Kaat did in the sixties and seventies.

Brecheen gained his greatest fame in the 1946 postseason. The Cardinals and Dodgers finished the regular season tied for first place in the National League, necessitating a best-of-three playoff. The first game was in St. Louis, where Pollett pitched a complete game and beat the Dodgers, 4–2. Games 2 and 3 were scheduled for Brooklyn.

Murry Dickson, a small right-hander, started Game 2 for the Cards, took a commanding 8–1 lead into the bottom of the ninth. But the Dodgers rallied and knocked Dickson from the box. Brecheen came in and gave up a single and a walk. That made it 8–4 and brought the tying run to the plate with one out. Brecheen then struck out Eddie Stanky and pinch-hitter Howie Schultz to nail down the victory and the pennant.

Four days later, Brecheen pitched a four-hit shutout to beat the Red Sox in Game 2 of the World Series. He started again in Game 6, pitched another complete game, and won, 4–1, to even the Series at three games apiece.

Dickson was the starter for the Cardinals in Game 7. He pitched into the eighth inning when he faltered and was relieved by Brecheen, who came back after only one day off. Harry gave up the tying run, which was charged to Dickson, then retired the side. It was in the bottom of the inning when Enos Slaughter made his famous mad dash from first to score what turned out to be the winning run. Brecheen was credited with his third victory of the Series and became the first left-hander to win three games in a World Series.

Had it not been for Warren Spahn, **Howie Pollet**, who had one of the great change-ups in baseball and who ranks third on my list, probably would have been considered the dominant left-handed pitcher in the National League in his time. He arrived in St. Louis in 1943 and was 8–4 with an earned run average of 1.75, leading the league despite the fact that his season was aborted when he was drafted into military service.

Pollet returned in 1946 and led the league with 21 wins and a 2.10 ERA, helping pitch the Cardinals to the National League pennant and the world championship. He won only 22 games over the next two seasons, but rebounded in 1949 with a 20–9 record, a 2.77 earned run average, and a league-leading five shutouts. It would be his last effective season. He spent the final six years of his career winning only 34 games with four different teams, but he remains a prominent name in Cardinals lore.

If Warren Spahn wasn't around, Howard Pollet would have been considered the best left-handed pitcher in the National League in the forties. *Allied Photo Color*

The sad fate of **Max Lanier** was to be persuaded by Jorge Pasquel to leave St. Louis and jump to the outlaw Mexican League. It was Pasquel's intention to form a league that would rival the major leagues. He started by stocking his teams with stars from the Negro Leagues before the major leagues broke the color line. He then raided the majors by waving lucrative contracts at established players who were grossly underpaid, especially in St. Louis. He managed to entice 23 players to leave the United States and go south of the border. Max Lanier was one of the 23.

My number four pick, Lanier had won 55 games for the Cardinals in four years and was 6–0 in 1946, when he packed up, took the money, and ran off to Mexico—a baseball elopement, but he married the wrong woman.

"Lanier had won 55 games for the Cardinals in four years and was 6–0 in 1946, when he packed up, took the money, and ran off to Mexico—a baseball elopement, but he married the wrong woman."

The Mexican League soon folded and those players who had jumped were suspended from organized baseball. The suspension was lifted in 1949 and Lanier returned to St. Louis, but his best years were behind him. He would win just 34 more games in five years with the Cardinals, the Giants, and the St. Louis Browns.

Lanier's son, Hal, an infielder, played in the big leagues for 10 seasons with the Giants and Yankees and later managed the Houston Astros to a division title.

John Tudor is fifth on my list. He had two tours of duty with the Cardinals. His best year was 1985, after he was traded by the Pirates to the Cards. He started the season 1–7, and then won 20 of his last 21 decisions.

Unfortunately for Tudor, Doc Gooden had a fabulous year for the Mets and John was deprived of the Cy Young Award. Tudor finished second to Gooden in ERA (1.53 to 1.93), second to Gooden in wins (24 to 21), second to Gooden in complete games (16 to 14), second to Gooden in innings pitched (277 to 275), and second to Gooden in the Cy Young voting. But he led the majors with 10 shutouts (two more than Gooden), and he had the satisfaction of beating Gooden's Mets, 1–0, in 10 innings in an important game in Shea Stadium during the September stretch run, one of the greatest baseball games ever played. And Tudor also had the satisfaction of pitching the Cardinals to a pennant and winning two games in the World Series against the Kansas City Royals, who beat the Cardinals in seven games.

The starting pitchers in the opening game of the 1943 World Series in Yankee Stadium were Spud Chandler (left) for the Yankees and Max Lanier for the Cardinals. The Yankees won the game, 4–2, and the Series, four games to one. *AP/Wide World Photos*

Tudor's career was cut short by an elbow injury, but while he was on the scene, he was one of the premier left-handers in the National League. John was a dart-thrower, a control specialist who got right-handed hitters out with sinkers down and away, out of the strike zone, and a paralyzing change-up.

In 1985, Tudor finished sixth in the National League in strikeouts and fourth in walks-to-innings-pitched, with 1.6 walks for every nine innings; precision pitching with a high strikeout total, a rarity among pitchers. That was John Tudor.

John Tudor led the National League with 10 shutouts in 1985 and then won two games in the World Series against Kansas City. *Lew Portnoy, Spectra-Action, Inc.*

Statistical Summaries

All statistics are for player's Cardinals career only.

PITCHING

G = Games

W = Games won

L = Games lost

PCT = Winning percentage

SHO = Shutouts

SO = Strikeouts

ERA = Earned run average

Left-Handed Pitcher	Years	G	W	L	PCT	SHO	SO	ERA
Steve Carlton *Struck out 19 batters in loss to Mets on September 15, 1969*	1965–71	190	77	62	.554	16	951	3.10
Harry Brecheen *Led N.L. in winning percentage, ERA, strikeouts, and shutouts in 1948*	1940 1943–52	292	128	79	.618	25	857	2.91
Howard Pollet *N.L. ERA leader in 1943 and 1946*	1941–43 1946–51	247	97	65	.599	20	635	3.06

(continued)	Years	G	W	L	PCT	SHO	SO	ERA
Max Lanier *Went 6–0 in six starts in 1946, all complete games*	1938–46 1949–51	277	101	69	.594	20	764	2.84
John Tudor *Last pitcher to have 10 shutouts in a season (1985)*	1985–88 1990	128	62	26	.705	12	448	2.52

FIELDING

PO = Put-outs

A = Assists

E = Errors

DP = Double plays

TC/G = Total chances divided by games played

FA = Fielding average

Left-Handed Pitcher	PO	A	E	DP	TC/G	FA
Steve Carlton	33	197	12	12	1.3	.950
Harry Brecheen	73	347	8	22	1.5	.981
Howard Pollet	45	263	14	24	1.3	.957
Max Lanier	64	283	14	20	1.3	.961
John Tudor	47	165	6	16	1.7	.972

ELEVEN

Relief Pitcher

I SOMETIMES WONDER IF **Bruce Sutter** has any idea what he started. Did Thomas Edison know what he started? Did Alexander Graham Bell? How about Doctor De Bakey?

Sutter didn't invent the split-finger fastball, but he popularized it and spawned an entire generation of split-finger pitchers until it became *the* pitch of the late eighties.

The split-finger fastball had its origin in the earliest days of baseball. It's forebear was the "forkball," made popular in 1959 by Elroy Face when he won 18 games in relief for the Pittsburgh Pirates, lost only 1, and saved 10 others. The forkball and the split-finger are similar pitches, both held between the index and middle fingers, which are spread wide enough to fit a baseball. The distinction between the forkball and the splitter is that the splitter is held farther down toward the tips of the fingers; therefore, it is choked less and thrown harder.

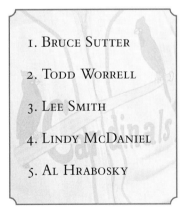

1. BRUCE SUTTER

2. TODD WORRELL

3. LEE SMITH

4. LINDY MCDANIEL

5. AL HRABOSKY

Roger Craig, who pitched for the Dodgers, Mets, Cardinals, Reds, and Phillies; coached for the Tigers; and managed the Giants, is credited with being the guru of the split-finger fastball because he advocated its use among his pitchers. But it was Sutter's success with the Cubs and Cardinals in the late seventies and early eighties that earned the split-finger fastball acceptance in the pitchers fraternity. Baseball, like a lot of industries, is notorious for jumping on a bandwagon and copying what is successful.

"If necessity is the mother of invention in science and construction, finding a way to stay in the major leagues is the grandmother of invention in baseball."

It's safe to say Sutter, my number one choice of Cards relief pitchers, would not have stayed in the big leagues were it not for the split-finger, just as the split-finger transformed Jack Morris from a good pitcher to a great pitcher.

If necessity is the mother of invention in science and construction, finding a way to stay in the major leagues is the grandmother of invention in baseball. A promising career was almost aborted when Sutter underwent arm surgery in 1973. He knew, after the surgery, that he would have to come up with another pitch if he was ever going to pitch in the big leagues. He tinkered with, and developed, the split-finger. It turned him into a dominant pitcher. His impact, because of the split-finger, was stunning.

Sutter was at the forefront in the sudden emergence into prominence of the late inning reliever, or closer, which is one of the biggest changes in the game over the past 30 years. In his second season, he won 7 games in relief for the Cubs, saved 31, and had an earned run average of 1.35. He led the league in saves in 1979 and 1980, and then was traded to the Cardinals for three players.

In St. Louis, Sutter picked up where he had left off in Chicago. He led the league in saves in three of the next four seasons, including a career high 45 in 1984.

That winter, Sutter signed a six-year, eight-figure free-agent contract with the Braves, but he would not play out that contract to its completion. Shoulder problems reduced his effectiveness and caused him to miss most of the 1986 season and all of 1987. In four seasons with the Braves, he saved only 40 games. When he retired, he was the all-time saves leader with 300.

Some pitchers are big and strong and look like they're throwing hard, but they really aren't. Not **Todd Worrell**. He was big (6′5½″, 222 pounds) and strong, and he threw as hard as it looked like he might. He was overpowering with a fastball in the 90-mile-an-hour-range and a hard slider, and he was a dominant closer for the Cards for a stretch of five years, during which he saved 121 games.

Worrell, ranked second on my list, was in the center of one of the lowest points in Cardinals history, a game that still sticks in the craw of long-time, die-hard Cards fans.

It was Game 6 of the 1985 World Series against the Kansas City Royals. The Cards led the Series, three games to two, and took a 1–0 lead into the

Before it was fashionable, Bruce Sutter used the split-finger fastball to become the dominant closer of the eighties. *Lew Portnoy, Spectra-Action, Inc.*

Todd Worrell threw hard—like a 6'5½" and 225-pound man, which he was. *Lew Portnoy, Spectra-Action, Inc.*

bottom of the ninth inning. With Worrell coming in to pitch, the Cards seemed on the verge of nailing down their ninth world championship.

Worrell, a rookie, had emerged late in the season as the Cardinals' closer. He had saved Game 1 for John Tudor with two-and-a-third innings of one-hit relief, and he had come back in Game 5 to pitch two innings, facing six batters and striking out all six. Now, he was asked to get three more outs and nail down the championship.

Veteran Jorge Orta, a pinch-hitter, led off the bottom of the ninth with a slow roller to the right side, fielded by first baseman Jack Clark. His flip to Worrell, covering first, seemed to be in time to get Orta, but first-base umpire Don Denkinger called the runner safe. The Cardinals argued to no avail. (Television replays would confirm that Worrell had touched first base before Orta's foot hit the bag and the runner should have been called out.)

The next batter, Steve Balboni, hit a foul pop that Clark failed to catch. With a second life, Balboni singled to left, putting Royals on first and second with none out. The Cards breathed easier when Jim Sundberg bunted and Orta was forced at third. But a passed ball by Darrell Porter put the tying run on third and the winning run on second. Hal McRae was then intentionally walked to load the bases, but pinch-hitter Dane Iorg looped one into right center that fell for a hit. Two runs scored and the Royals had won Game 6, 2–1.

In Game 7, the Royals teed off on Tudor. They scored two in the second and knocked him out with three more in the third. Then they put up a six spot in the fifth and, with Bret Saberhagen breezing on a five-hitter, the Royals won Game 7, 11–0, and took the World Series away from the Cardinals—a bitter pill for Cards' fans to swallow.

After the 1992 season, Worrell left St. Louis to sign a free-agent contract with the Dodgers and continued to be a dominant closer, saving 111 games in a three-year stretch. Then, like Sutter, Worrell had arm problems that shortened his career.

Lee Smith was even bigger than Todd Worrell (6′6″, 245 pounds) and threw just as hard. He had a remarkable career in the sense that he pitched for 18 years, which is unusual for a relief pitcher, and was a dominant closer for four teams, the Cubs, Cardinals, Red Sox, and Angels. He saved 30 or more games for four straight years and had more than 40 saves four times in his career, including a high of 47 for the Cardinals in 1991.

He was big and he threw hard: Lee Smith had more saves than any other pitcher in baseball history. *AP/Wide World Photos*

Smith is baseball's all-time saves leader with 478, but only 160 of them were with the Cardinals, which is why he's only third on my all-time list of Cardinals relievers.

Unfortunately for **Lindy McDaniel**, he came along too soon to be recognized for what he was, one of the great relief pitchers ever. A change in the rules—more important a change in the philosophy of the use of relief pitchers—kept McDaniel from compiling the saves total that would have earned him his just due.

Most of McDaniel's career was before 1969, when saves became an official statistic of major league baseball. Eventually, statisticians researched every box score in the history of the game, applied the requirements for a save, and updated the save totals for every relief pitcher. But it stands to reason that with no saves records kept prior to 1969, they had not yet become ammunition to be used in contract negotiations, and relievers had little incentive to compile them.

Over the years, the role of the relief pitcher has changed dramatically. There was a time when the relief pitcher was a veteran who could no longer go nine innings. Until the seventies, there were only a handful of relief specialists who distinguished themselves. Their identity was yet to emerge. By the seventies, however, there was a proliferation of relief pitchers. They became vital parts of pitching staffs, specialists who were called on to get out of tough situations in the late innings. With each succeeding decade, the relief pitcher became more important, more specialized to the point that today a dominant closer is essential to a championship team.

"With each succeeding decade the relief pitcher became more important, more specialized, to the point that today a dominant closer is essential to a championship team."

In baseball's early days, there was a higher premium placed on the complete game than there is today. Pitchers were expected to finish what they started. Now, the attitude is that if you get six good innings out of your starter, he's done his job, and the manager can then turn the game over to his bullpen.

For example, in 1920, when there were only eight teams in each league, the National League had 694 complete games. In 1955, McDaniel's first season, there were 385 complete games in the National League, still with eight teams.

By 1980, in a 12-team league, the number of complete games in the National League had dropped to 307. And in the 2000 season, the National League, now with 16 teams, had only 127 complete games.

In McDaniel's day, a manager might bring his closer into the game in the eighth inning, even the seventh and, on rare occasions, the sixth, to choke off a rally. He usually would come in with runners on base, the game on the line. Today's closers are usually brought in only in the ninth inning, often to start the inning and without regard to how effective the previous pitcher, starter or middleman, had been. A starter may have pitched eight shutout innings; the closer will still be brought in to start the ninth.

Lindy McDaniel pitched 21 years in the major leagues, most of them as a reliever, and recorded only 172 saves. I strongly believe that operating under

Before the relief pitcher burst into prominence, and before saves became an official baseball statistic, Lindy McDaniel, whose brother Von also pitched for the Cardinals, finished off many victories for the Cards. *Allied Photo Color*

today's philosophy regarding the use of relievers, he could have at least doubled that number. I rate him fourth of all-time Cardinals relievers.

Rounding out the top five is **Al Hrabosky**, one of the best relief pitchers of the seventies and one of baseball's most colorful characters of any era. They called him the "Mad Hungarian." The name came from his heritage and from his antics on the mound.

It was in the late sixties and seventies, remember, when long hair and facial hair became all the rage with baseball players. The Oakland Athletics started it when their maverick owner, Charles O. Finley, offered each member of the team $300 if they would grow mustaches. It soon spread to other teams, and Hrabosky grew this huge Fu Manchu mustache and had long hair that flowed out from the back of his cap.

Al used the long hair and Fu Manchu as affectations to present a menacing figure on the mound, and he embellished them by scowling at hitters and with a ritual that became his trademark. Before each pitch, he would walk behind the mound, turn his back to the hitter, bow his head, and talk to himself; then he would slam the ball into his glove and turn around with a flourish and face the hitter with a scowl.

Hrabosky said this ritual came about early in his career with the Cardinals. Actually, he said he used a variation of the ritual when he was a starting pitcher in the minor leagues. Between innings, after he had taken his warm-up pitches and the ball was being tossed around the infield, Al would stomp around the mound talking to himself to get pumped up for the next inning.

When he got to the Cardinals, he had been converted into a relief pitcher, but he was having a rough time. He was on the verge of being sent back to the minor leagues, and he was brought into a one-sided game when he began to realize his career was on the line. So Al reverted to his minor league practice and began stomping around the mound and talking to himself. That's when the whole Mad Hungarian act began.

And that's all it was, an act. Hrabosky knew it. The opposition knew it. And Al knew they knew it, but he figured it was just one more thing he could put into a hitter's head.

I remember something Gene Mauch, one of the sharpest baseball minds I've ever been around, once told me. Gene was always yelling from the bench, causing distractions, doing things to get under the skin of opposing

With his long hair, Fu Manchu mustache, and intimidating scowl, Al Hrabosky, the "Mad Hungarian," was a menacing figure on the mound. *Lew Portnoy, Spectra-Action, Inc.*

players. He said if his taunting and his antics got a reaction from an opposing player, then he earned an advantage.

"If one guy on the other team thinks about me instead of what he's supposed to be doing," Mauch used to say, "then I've done my job because he shouldn't be thinking about me. Not for a second."

It was the same with Hrabosky. If a hitter was thinking about, distracted by, or enraged by the Mad Hungarian act, he was giving Al an advantage. I used to laugh at that stuff. I never took it seriously, and I don't think Hrabosky did either. Believe me, it wasn't his act that made him such a good relief pitcher, it was his fastball.

One day when I was with the Phillies, we were having a horrible time against Hrabosky and our manager, Danny Ozark, a wonderful man famous for his malaprops, stood up in the dugout and tried to rally his troops.

"The Mad Hungarian," Danny said. "Come on, let's send this guy back to Hungaria."

Picking the five best Cardinals relief pitchers is no easy matter. The greatest in the game have worn the Cardinals uniform, and another almost did. Think about it. Among them, Lee Smith, Dennis Eckersley, Tom Henke, Bruce Sutter, and Todd Worrell, all Cardinals at one time during their careers, had a combined total of 1,735 saves. It's staggering! And Hall of Famer Rollie Fingers, with 341 saves, was a Cardinal for four days, but never wore a Redbirds uniform. Fingers was traded to the Cardinals by the San Diego Padres as part of an 11-player trade on December 8, 1980. Four days later, Fingers went from the Cards to the Milwaukee Brewers as part of a 7-player trade.

Statistical Summaries

All statistics are for player's Cardinals career only.

PITCHING

G = Games

W = Games won

L = Games lost

PCT = Winning percentage

SV = Saves

SO = Strikeouts

ERA = Earned run average

Relief Pitcher	Years	G	W	L	PCT	SV	SO	ERA
Bruce Sutter *Had a win and two saves in 1982 World Series vs. Brewers*	1981–84	249	26	30	.464	127	259	2.72
Todd Worrell *Struck out record six straight Royals in Game 5 of 1985 World Series*	1985–89 1992	348	33	33	.500	129	365	2.56
Lee Smith *Had over 40 saves a season from 1991 to 1993*	1990–93	245	15	20	.429	160	246	2.90

(continued)	Years	G	W	L	PCT	SV	SO	ERA
Lindy McDaniel *Allowed just 85 hits in 116⅓ innings pitched in 1960*	1955–62	336	66	54	.550	64	523	3.88
Al Hrabosky *Had combined 21–4 record in 1974 and 1975*	1970–77	329	40	20	.667	59	385	2.93

FIELDING

Statistics are for player's entire career.

PO = Put-outs

A = Assists

E = Errors

DP = Double plays

TC/G = Total chances divided by games played

FA = Fielding average

Relief Pitcher	PO	A	E	DP	TC/G	FA
Bruce Sutter	38	61	3	3	0.4	.971
Todd Worrell	13	48	2	5	0.2	.968
Lee Smith	6	15	1	1	0.1	.955
Lindy McDaniel	55	185	9	14	0.7	.964
Al Hrabosky	10	39	6	3	0.2	.891

TWELVE

Manager

OTHER CARDINALS MANAGERS served in that capacity longer, won more games, won more pennants, and won more World Series, but **Whitey Herzog**, by the sheer force of his personality and his penchant for innovation, gets my vote as the greatest manager in Cardinals history.

When he arrived in St. Louis in 1980, Herzog had managed at two previous stops, one year in Texas and five in Kansas City, where he finished second twice and won three consecutive American League West titles, 1976–77–78, each time losing to the Yankees in the American League Championship Series.

1. WHITEY HERZOG

2. TONY LARUSSA

3. RED SCHOENDIENST

4. BILLY SOUTHWORTH

5. JOHNNY KEANE

When Herzog came to them, the Cardinals were in the throes of an 11-year drought. Although they managed to be competitive, they had not won a pennant since 1968. Herzog's impact was almost immediate. He succeeded Ken Boyer and interim manager Jack Krol on June 9 with the Cardinals at 18–34. By August 29 he had a record of 38–35, and he was kicked upstairs into the general manager's office. After the season, Herzog took over the dual role of general manager and field manager.

A players strike rocked baseball in 1981. The season was played in two halves; the Cardinals had the best overall record in the National League East, but they finished second in each half and, thus, were out of the playoffs. The following year, Herzog relinquished the general manager's job, concentrated on managing, and led the Cards to their first National League pennant in 14 years and their first World Series title since 1967. He managed in St. Louis

As an innovator, a motivator, and a tactician, Whitey Herzog was second to none among Cardinals managers. *Lew Portnoy, Spectra-Action, Inc.*

for eight more seasons, won two more pennants, and was replaced in 1990 by Joe Torre.

Known as the "White Rat," a sobriquet that was both affectionate and snide, Herzog could mix in a little nastiness with a little genius. He was ruthlessly efficient, and I say that admiringly, not ruthlessly. Once, at a team meeting, Whitey told Keith Hernandez, "Keith, I want you to get up in front of your teammates and tell them why you don't run balls out."

Imagine how devastating that would be for a player to hear in front of the whole team. How humiliating!

But Herzog was brilliant as a tactician. He was brilliant in his preparation, brilliant in the way he tailored his team to the ballpark he played in. In Kansas City, on artificial turf, Herzog made sure he had speed in the outfield with Willie Wilson and Amos Otis, who cut down doubles and triples in the gap. He did the same thing when he went to St. Louis, which also had artificial turf. He had speed in the outfield, and his shrewdness in molding a team is one of the biggest reasons the Cardinals won in 1982, 1985, and 1987.

Some baseball people have an eye for individual talent. Others have more of an overview of what it takes to win, an eye for team talent, if you will. Whitey had both, but he excelled in evaluating the sum rather than the parts. He had served as farm director for the Mets and helped put together the team that won the World Series in 1969. As general manager of the Cardinals, he made the trade for Bruce Sutter, who helped the Cardinals win the World Series in 1982. He also traded for Ozzie Smith, Lonnie Smith, Willie McGee, and Joaquin Andujar. He had the knack of taking a player of lesser talent, inserting him into the nucleus of the team, and making the team stronger.

Chuck Tanner was an innovative guy who first espoused the idea of using three pitchers in a game, a starter, a middleman and a closer, each with a specific, defined role. Herzog adopted that concept and took it one step further. It's done a lot today, but Herzog, more than any other manager, was the first to stack his bullpen with three left-handers and three right-handers and match them up against hitters.

Keith Hernandez once told me he never saw Herzog bring in a pitcher one hitter too late. Whitey considered six innings a complete game. After the sixth, he would match up left-handed pitcher against left-handed hitter, right-handed pitcher against right-handed hitter. And he would do that pretty much until the last out. When he lost Sutter, the individual, he used his bullpen, or group, as one.

Tony LaRussa is intelligent. Not because I say so. Not because he says so. Because his sheepskin says so. He has a degree from Florida State University School of Law and is a member of the bar, one of five managers in baseball history who were lawyers. The others, Monte Ward, Hughie Jennings, Miller Huggins, and Branch Rickey all are in the Hall of Fame.

Along the way, LaRussa picked up a reputation for being a guy who manages by computer. He uses computers, sure. It's a sign of the times. But he's more than just a Microsoft manager. His success is the result of exemplary

Tony LaRussa is one of five managers in baseball history to hold a law degree. He's second on my list of all-time Cardinals managers and still adding to his illustrious career. *AP/Wide World Photos*

preparation and attention to detail. He's often accused of overmanaging. I don't share that opinion. I believe the reason for the accusations is Tony is so bright, and overt intelligence in baseball is often looked upon as a shortcoming rather than an asset. "Too smart for his own good" is a common criticism. But Tony has backed it up by being successful with three different teams. He won with the Chicago White Sox (a division title in 1983), with the Oakland A's (American League pennants in 1988–89–90, World Series champion in 1989), and with the Cardinals (division titles in 1996, 2000, and 2002).

Furthermore, LaRussa and his longtime pitching coach, Dave Duncan, revived the careers of both Dave Stewart and Dennis Eckersley in Oakland. To my mind, LaRussa and Duncan don't get the credit they deserve, at least not for those two reclamation projects. LaRussa comes in second on my all-time list.

When **Red Schoendienst** took over as manager of the Cardinals in 1965 (he had been a coach under Johnny Keane), he realized he had a team made up of strong personalities—Bob Gibson, Dal Maxvill, Mike Shannon, Curt Flood, Dick Groat, Lou Brock—and he was smart enough to leave well enough alone.

Red, who takes the number three slot on my list, is one of the nicest people in the world, and that's how he was as a manager. He was like a member of the family, an uncle or an older brother, and his approach to managing was fatherly or avuncular. He would come out for a meeting at the mound and he'd look around at Cepeda, Maxie, Shannon, or me and say, "What do you guys want to do?"

He won back-to-back pennants in 1967 and 1968, which hadn't been done by a Cardinals manager in a quarter of a century, and his 12-year tenure (1965–1976) is the longest of any Cardinals manager.

Red is the consummate organizational man with more than 60 years in the game, most of them with the Cardinals as a player, coach, manager, and special assistant to the general manager. Two years after he was fired as manager of the Cardinals, he came back to coach under Ken Boyer and served as a coach under Whitey Herzog and Joe Torre until Red moved to the front office. Twice he was asked to take over the team as interim manager.

It takes a special man to do that, a man completely devoid of ego. A man like Red Schoendienst.

Red Schoendienst was our manager on the Cardinals National League pennant-winning teams of 1967 and 1968. *AP/Wide World Photos*

172

I never knew my number four pick, **Billy Southworth**, but I feel as if I did from everything I've heard about him from Stan Musial and Red Schoendienst, who played for him and thought very highly of him.

Southworth was a taskmaster as a manager and a controversial figure. As a player, he was a left-handed hitting outfielder, a little guy who dated back to 1913 and played with the Indians, Pirates, Braves, Giants, and Cardinals.

Southworth began his managing career in 1928 with the Cardinals' International League farm team in Rochester. The following year he replaced Bill McKechnie as manager of the Cardinals. He was such a martinet and caused so much dissension on the team, the players almost started a mutiny. Billy was fired and returned to the farm team in Rochester, where he won three consecutive pennants.

But Southworth remained persona non grata with the Cardinals and was let go. He coached for the New York Giants until the Cardinals brought him back to the organization in 1935. Eventually, he worked his way back up and was made manager of the Cardinals again in 1940.

Yankees manager Joe McCarthy (left) and Cardinals manager Billy Southworth opposed each other in the World Series of 1942, won by the Cardinals in five games, and 1943, won by the Yankees in five games. *AP/Wide World Photos*

More mature this time, he toned down his demanding style and brought the team in second in 1941. He then won three consecutive pennants, in 1942–43–44, the only Cardinals manager to win three straight pennants, and topped it off with World Series championships in 1942 and 1944.

"If ever a man was etched into a position to manage the Cardinals, it was Keane. His style as a manager was patriarchal, what you might expect from someone who once thought about studying for the priesthood."

The Cardinals finished second under Southworth in 1945, but the following year a $50,000 offer lured him to Boston, where, in 1948, he led the Braves to their first pennant in 34 years.

Southworth managed in the major leagues with the Cardinals and Braves for 13 seasons and only once finished in the second division.

Midway through the 1961 season, with the team in sixth place, eight games under .500, the Cardinals fired Solly Hemus as manager and replaced him with **Johnny Keane**, one of his coaches. Under Keane, the man who is fifth on my list, the Cardinals were marginally improved in the second half of the season.

If ever a man was etched into a position to manage the Cardinals, it was Keane. His style as a manager was patriarchal, what you might expect from someone who once thought about studying for the priesthood. He was soft-spoken and low-key, a genuinely nice man.

Johnny never played in the major leagues, but he became a manager in the Cardinals' farm system at a young age and managed in the minor leagues for more than 20 years. He spent his entire career in the Cardinals organization and was brought to the big club as a coach under Hemus in 1959.

Through the years, Keane built a strong relationship with Bing Devine, who had worked his way up the ranks to become the Cardinals' general manager, and it was Devine who made Keane the manager when Hemus was fired.

St. Louis finished sixth in 1962, but in 1963 Keane had us in contention until the final two weeks of the season. We ended up second to the Los Angeles Dodgers by six games.

During one stretch in September, the Cardinals won 19 of 20 games before an epic three-game series in St. Louis against the Dodgers. The Dodgers came in with a one-game lead. Johnny Podres and Sandy Koufax allowed just one run in the first two games, and Dick Nen, father of San Francisco Giants closer Robb Nen, hit a pinch-hit home run during the top of the ninth inning of the third game to tie the score. The Dodgers won in extra innings, swept this remarkable series, and left the Gateway City four games up.

The 1964 season began with high hopes and wound up producing the greatest pennant race in National League history.

After he guided the Cardinals to the pennant in 1964, Johnny Keane quit as manager. The next year he replaced Yogi Berra as manager of the Yankees—miscast with a strange team in a strange league. He lasted only a little more than one season. *Bettman/CORBIS*

The Phillies looked like a lock to win it. With two weeks to go, they led by 6½ games. Then, suddenly, the Phillies went into a nosedive, losing 10 straight games. They couldn't buy a win, and three other contenders, the Reds, the Giants, and the Cardinals, kept winning, cutting into Philly's lead. Going into the final weekend of the season, three teams still had a chance to win the pennant. We lost the first two games of a three-game series with the Mets. In the final game that Sunday, Bob Gibson, who had pitched a complete game on Friday night, relieved Curt Simmons in the fifth inning and pitched into the ninth when Barney Schultz got the last two outs. Gibson got the win, the Reds lost to the Phillies, and we were National League champions.

It may sound strange to say that winning a pennant caused a franchise embarrassment, but that pretty much sums up the situation in St. Louis. On August 23, when it looked like the Phillies would win going away, the Cardinals were 11½ games back. They fired Bing Devine, the general manager whose trade in June for Lou Brock won the pennant for us, and replaced him with Bob Howsam. But it was Branch Rickey, who had been brought in as president, who was calling the shots.

Keane was Devine's guy and with Bing gone, Johnny's job was also in jeopardy. Rickey wanted to bring in Leo Durocher for the stretch run as kind of a jolt to turn the team around. In fact, Rickey and Durocher had agreed on a deal that Durocher would replace Keane after the season. But the Cardinals started winning, creeping closer and closer to Philadelphia.

Keane resented Rickey's interference. Johnny had seemingly saved his job by winning the pennant, but he was a man of principle, and he would let his principle and his resentment of Rickey get in the way of his judgment.

Our opponent in the World Series was the Yankees, who, like the Cardinals, looked like a beaten team in August. But, also like us, the Yankees closed with a rush and won the pennant under their rookie manager, Yogi Berra.

We won the Series in seven games, and what followed was one of the most bizarre events in baseball history. Two days after the seventh game, the Yankees fired Berra. A few weeks later, they announced they had hired Johnny Keane as their manager. Ralph Houk, who had left the field as manager and had taken over as general manager of the Yankees after the 1963 season, had managed against Keane in the American Association and had always admired Johnny's style. It was Houk who hired Keane to replace Berra. So, here you had the two World Series managers leaving the team each had led to a pennant, one pushed out, the other leaving of his own volition. I'm telling you, it was bizarre!

Keane's tenure with the Yankees was a disaster. And it was brief. He had taken over a team that was growing old rapidly. Roger Maris was hurt most of the 1965 season. Mickey Mantle and Whitey Ford were quickly coming to the end of their fabulous careers. And the underrated Tony Kubek had decided that season would be his last.

In addition, Keane was completely miscast as manager of the Yankees. He had spent 31 years—his entire professional career—with the Cardinals organization and now, with the Yankees, he was a foreigner. He didn't know the organization. He didn't know the players. He didn't know the American League.

The Yankees tumbled from first place in 1964 under Berra to sixth in 1965 under Keane. The following year, when the Yankees won only 4 of their first 20 games, Keane was fired. Ralph Houk came down from the front office and put the uniform back on to manage the team.

In 1966 Keane was out of baseball for the first time in more than three decades. He died of a heart attack the following January at the age of 55.

Statistical Summaries

All statistics are for manager's Cardinals career only.

MANAGING

G = Games managed

W = Games won

L = Games lost

PCT = Winning percentage

P = Pennants

WS = World Series victories

Manager	Years	G	W	L	PCT	P	WS
Whitey Herzog *Won five division titles with Royals and Cards*	1980–90	1,551	822	878	.530	3	1
Tony LaRussa *Most victories of managers active in 2002 (1,924)*	1996–2002	1,133	604	529	.533	0	0
Red Schoendienst *Holds 2–0 record as N.L. All-Star Game manager in 1967 and 1968 (46–18)*	1965–76 1980 1990	1,999	1,041	955	.522	2	1

(continued)	Years	G	W	L	PCT	P	WS
Billy Southworth *Has fifth highest overall winning percentage (.595 with Cards and Braves*	1929 1940–45	981	620	346	.642	3	2
Johnny Keane *Had a winning record each season with Cards*	1961–64	567	317	249	.560	1	1

Index